"צדיק באמונתו יחיה"

May the stories and concepts in this special book inspire you and lift your spirits on those more difficult days.
With Hashem in our lives the possibilities are infinite....
remember to open the door and let Him in.....
Wishing you a relaxing and well-deserved summer break!

Love,
Mrs. Gross and Dr. Rosenberg
Valley Torah High School
June 16, 2022

ArtScroll® Series

Rabbi Nosson Scherman / Rabbi Gedaliah Zlotowitz

General Editors

Rabbi Meir Zlotowitz ז״ל, *Founder and President*

Living

Published by
ARTSCROLL®
Mesorah Publications, ltd

VOLUME 2
of the best-selling teen series

ALON FAMILY EDITION

Emunah FOR TEENS 2

Achieving a life of serenity through faith

Rabbi David Ashear

Adapted by Chana Nestlebaum

FIRST EDITION
Five Impressions ... April 2021

Published and Distributed by
MESORAH PUBLICATIONS, LTD.
313 Regina Avenue / Rahway, N.J. 07065

Distributed in Europe by
LEHMANNS
Unit E, Viking Business Park
Rolling Mill Road
Jarow, Tyne & Wear, NE32 3DP
England

Distributed in Australia and New Zealand
by **GOLDS WORLDS OF JUDAICA**
3-13 William Street
Balaclava, Melbourne 3183
Victoria, Australia

Distributed in Israel by
SIFRIATI / A. GITLER — BOOKS
POB 2351
Bnei Brak 51122

Distributed in South Africa by
KOLLEL BOOKSHOP
Northfield Centre, 17 Northfield Avenue
Glenhazel 2192, Johannesburg, South Africa

ARTSCROLL® SERIES
LIVING EMUNAH FOR TEENS
VOLUME 2

ITEM CODE: LEMT2H

ISBN 10: 1-4226-2872-2 / ISBN 13: 978-1-4226-2872-0

Typography by CompuScribe at ArtScroll Studios, Ltd.

Printed in the United States of America
Bound by Sefercraft, Quality Bookbinders, Ltd., Rahway, N.J. 07065

We are privileged to dedicate this volume on *emunah* in memory of our beloved husband and father, who personified *emunah*,

Rabbi Moshe Alon ז״ל

הרב משה בן שלמה ז״ל

9 Nissan 5777

In the year and era of Covid, lockdown, fear, and economic privation, how can people remain strong and cope with a crisis beyond their control? The answer is one word: *Emunah*!

Our father epitomized *emunah*. He lived with it. It infused his *tefillah*, his learning, his business activity, his dealings with others, his integrity. When times were good, he thanked Hashem. When times were hard, he had total faith that whatever Hashem decrees is ultimately good. His life remains a lesson for us and all who knew him.

It is so appropriate, therefore, that we honor his memory with this book that conveys his essence to Klal Yisrael's precious young people. May his example continue to be an inspiration to others as it is to us.

Mrs. Osnas Alon
and children

Table of Contents

Introduction

Even if this year were a year like any other, a book that offers new insights and ideas about *emunah* would be well worth writing. After all, if we tune in to our *neshamah,* we can hear it telling us constantly, "I'm thirsty!" — and only *emunah* can satisfy its thirst. Just as we need more water every day, even if yesterday we drank our fill, we also need more inspiration for our *emunah* every day, even if we've already learned a great deal on this subject. Therefore, we are pleased and grateful to be able to present you with the second volume of *Living Emunah for Teens.*

On another level, this book comes out at a unique moment in history, the likes of which we have never seen before. We hope that by the time these words are in print, Hashem will have healed the world from the terrible pandemic that has taken so many of *Klal Yisrael's* illustrious individuals, devastated families, and thrown the world's economy into chaos. We hope that the light of *Geulah* will already be shining brightly, and that the lessons of *emunah* we teach in this book will already be obvious for all to see.

However, we also recognize that Hashem runs the world according to His own calculations and therefore, we might still be living under the cloud of *galus.* In that case, the lessons in this book are more important than ever. Only with a strong belief that Hashem is our loving Father and that EVERYTHING is for our good can we overcome the worry and fear that times like this can stir in our hearts.

You may wonder, "How can all the bad news we've been hearing and seeing with our own eyes *not* shake our belief that Hashem loves us?" The answer lines in two words: *Avinu Malkeinu* — our Father, our King.

Some people relate to Hashem very much as the King — the All-Powerful Being Who scrutinizes our every move and punishes those who don't obey Him. Just as they might keep their distance from a strict principal or a grouchy neighbor, they "keep their distance" from Hashem. They do what they have to do to satisfy Him and try their best not to "get in His way."

But when we serve Hashem in this way, our relationship is a cold and distant one. It offers us neither comfort nor security. *Avinu,* our Father, loves us! Yes, He is the King, but the King is our Father. A king's child doesn't try to avoid his father; he is secure in knowing that the very same individual who has all the power also loves him in a special way. That means that whatever this child needs, he will be given. His father has the kingdom's whole treasury at his fingertips and because he loves his son with all his heart, there's nothing he won't do to help him.

That's our Father, our King.

But you might say, "What about when the son disobeys the king? Is he still willing to help him? Maybe then, he will punish him."

That's where the difference between a human king and the King of kings becomes evident. A human king has an ego. He's offended personally when his authority is threatened. He might indeed punish someone — even his own son — for offending his honor. Hashem, however, does not have an ego. He has only love and kindness. When He sends troubles our way, it's only meant to steer us and our world onto the right path, the path that will lead to the *Geulah* He has promised. In that process, as individuals and as a *klal,* we experience suffering. Never, though, can we think for a moment that our suffering is Hashem's purpose.

> *A mashal: Zev finally got his driver's license. His father, a wealthy man, had a powerful sports car parked in the garage and Zev couldn't wait to take it for a spin. He had been promising his friends that as soon as he was allowed to drive, he would take them all on a ride along an empty country road outside his neighborhood.*

Now, on a fine summer day, Zev stood in his driveway holding his long-awaited license as his two friends took turns admiring it.

"When are we taking out your father's car?" asked one.

"Ummm, I'm not sure. He's at work now, so I can't ask him," Zev answered. But as he took note of his friends' disappointed faces, he had a thought. "You know, I kind of already asked him once if I could try his car when I got my license, and he said it would be OK, so I'm sure it's still OK."

Zev ran into his house and brought out his father's spare keys that were kept on a hook near the door. The boys piled into the car and were soon zooming freely along the winding road with the windows down and the music playing. Suddenly, the road took a sharp turn and Zev, taken by surprise and too inexperienced to react skillfully, slammed the car into a tree.

In moments, the ambulance was there. The passengers were only slightly injured, but Zev was in serious condition. He was brought straight into the emergency room. The head physician, who came rushing to the patient's side, was none other than Zev's father.

Zev had done the wrong thing by taking his father's car without permission. But was his father about to scold him for it? Of course not. He would do everything he could to help his precious son! In the same way, when Hashem sees us making mistakes, He says, as it were, "My child is hurting himself so badly and he doesn't even realize what he's doing. I need to help him find the right path." Our sins against Hashem may lead us to "crash," but His response is not to punish but rather, to do everything to help us.

This is sometimes a difficult thought to hold onto when we experience pain or disappointment. Imagine how the Jewish people felt when they saw the Beis HaMikdash in ruins; Hashem had literally abandoned His home among His people. The navi Yeshayah (49:14) tells us that "the people said Hashem has abandoned and forgotten me." But in the very next pasuk, Hashem reassures them that

He can no more forget them than a mother can forget the baby she carries inside her. In other words, Hashem sees us as a part of Him: "The Jewish nation and Hashem are one."

The more we learn and understand the depth of Hashem's love for us, the more we will want to become closer to Him. Yesterday's relationship will seem too shallow for the increased love we have today, and tomorrow will bring an even greater level as we keep satisfying our *neshamah's* thirst for *emunah.*

There is a well-known story of Rav Saadia Gaon that illustrates how our *emunah* can deepen day by day. He had been traveling, and stopped for the night at the home of a kindhearted Jew who welcomed guests. The host treated the Rav warmly, fed him well, and made sure he was comfortable. When it was time to leave, Rav Saadia thanked the host and went on his way. Soon, the Rav saw the host running after him calling out, "Wait! Rabbi! Please forgive me!" Rav Saadia assured the man that there was nothing to forgive. He had taken great care of his guest. "But I didn't know who you were," the man answered. "Had I realized, I would have shown you much more honor!"

Based on this experience, Rav Saadia adopted the practice of doing *teshuvah* every day for treating Hashem with insufficient respect. Why? It was because every day, he discovered a little more about Who Hashem is and what He was doing for him, and therefore, yesterday's level of honor was not enough.

You can visualize how this might apply to your own life. Imagine that it's your birthday and your mother bakes you a cake. You're delighted and give her a big thank-you. But the next day, your sister tells you that your mother had to walk to three stores to find the special ingredients she needed for the cake and worked for an hour to get the decorations on it just right. Now your big thank-you seems nowhere big enough.

There is so much we don't know about Hashem and what He does for us. Every time we recognize another way in which He guides us and shows us His love, we should feel inspired to come closer to Him. *B'ezras Hashem,* the lessons you are about to learn will open your eyes every day to another kindness, another gift, another way in which Hashem is helping you to grow and refine yourself and find your greatness. And with that, may every day bring you to a greater height of love for Hashem and trust in His constant kindness.

1

Be Simple

Don't try to "figure out" Hashem.

Zaidy was very sick. He lay in a hospital bed, a strained expression on his face, a mass of tubes connected to various parts of his body. Zehava's mother stood with her at the bedside. They spoke to him about happy news and he listened, half-asleep.

"Is he going to die?" Zehava asked her mother fearfully as they walked back to the hospital elevator. She was only 12. She had never lost anyone she loved, and there were few people in the world whom she loved as much as her Zaidy. She hated seeing him suffering. He didn't deserve it!

"Keep davening," her mother told her. "Zaidy is not in good shape, but Hashem can do anything."

And so Zehava prayed for Zaidy. She prayed for him in Shemoneh Esrei, she said Tehillim for him, she did mitzvos in his merit. She launched an all-out save Zaidy campaign, but two weeks into her campaign, Zaidy passed away.

"How could Hashem do this to me?" she sobbed. "How could He ignore all my tefillos? I trusted Hashem and I davened with all my heart. It doesn't work!"

When we want something with all our heart and *daven* with all our strength, we become very close to Hashem. We put our trust in Him and believe that He will take care of our needs. But sometimes, the answer we hope for is not the answer we are given. Then, we may feel like someone whose friend has betrayed him: "I counted on Him and He let me down. He could have helped me but He didn't."

How do we maintain our *emunah* in such a situation? A person whose trust in Hashem is complete will not be shaken because he knows that Hashem's response is always the one that is best for him. With complete *emunah,* Zehava would realize that this was her Zaidy's time to leave the world and that the suffering he experienced during his illness was a *kapparah* that would bring him to Heaven with a clean, pure soul. She would be sad about losing someone she loved, and would cry because she missed him. However, she would not feel the awful sense of being abandoned by Hashem.

The cause of Zehava's *emunah* crisis is that she believes she can figure out Hashem. She thinks that Hashem operates according to certain rules, and when the results don't seem to line up with those rules, she no longer feels that she knows Hashem. Her thinking has gone wrong in one important way, which is that no human being can "figure out" Hashem. Shlomo HaMelech, whose wisdom was greater than anyone else's, tells us (*Koheles* 8:14) that we will never be able to understand why righteous people suffer because, as *Yeshayah* (55:8) states, "Hashem's thoughts are not like our thoughts, and His ways are not like our ways."

Our role is not to understand Hashem, but to trust Him in a simple way, like an infant trusts his mother. We can emulate Yaakov Avinu, the *ish tam* — simple man. This is not "simple" as in unintelligent, but rather, as in pure. Yaakov went to Charan with Hashem's guarantee that "I will guard you wherever you go," but soon found himself subject to Lavan's lies. Then he was confronted by Eisav and his army. Then his daughter Dina was kidnaped. And then, his beloved son Yosef was lost to him. Yet throughout his life, Yaakov never lost his trust in Hashem.

Mastering the art of simple trust is the major challenge we have in the final generation before Mashiach, the Ramchal states. When we see good people caught up in difficult circumstances, when we are confused by the events taking place all around us, this is the time to hold on even tighter to Hashem. It's time to stop trying to figure it out and just be simple.

MAKE IT REAL:

Practice telling yourself, "I don't have to understand — Hashem understands," when events seem unfair or confusing.

2

"How Did I Deserve All This?"

A humble heart is the key to tefillah.

When things go wrong, we often wonder, "Hashem, what did I do to deserve this? I try so hard!" We think of all the mitzvos we do, all the *tefillos* we've said, and we feel a bit cheated. But do we ever question Hashem's *hashgachah* when things go well? Do we ever think, "Hashem, I'm so small. I have so many flaws and make so many mistakes. Whatever I've accomplished has only been because You've helped me. What did I ever do to deserve so much kindness from You?"

We might not think that this is a good way to present ourselves before the Judge. Wouldn't we be better off highlighting our merits rather than confessing our weaknesses? Yaakov Avinu teaches us that in fact, approaching Hashem with humility — with a true realization of how much He gives us even though we cannot earn it or give Him anything in return — is the only sincere way to pray for what we need.

When Yaakov prays to Hashem to save him from Eisav, his first words are, "*Katonti mikol ha'chassadim* — I have been diminished by all the kindnesses...that You have done for Your servant" (*Bereishis* 32:11). He recognizes that Hashem has granted him exceptional wealth and *berachah*; he came to Lavan alone, and he is returning to Eretz Yisrael with so large a household that he has divided it into two camps. The feeling behind his prayer is, "Hashem, You've already given me so much more than I could possibly deserve, and still I'm asking You to please help me to face this challenge."

But is it not true that we do so much for Hashem? When we wake up early to get to *minyan* or pull ourselves away from our activities to *daven* Minchah, or rush home to be on time for Shabbos, or ignore our rumbling stomach on a fast day, or wear long-sleeved clothing on a hot day because it is proper as befits a Jew, aren't we deserving of reward?

The answer to that question comes from realizing how much good a mitzvah does us. We are the ones who benefit, more than we can ever imagine. When Hashem gives us an opportunity to do a mitzvah, He is handing us the key to a vault full of *berachah* in this world and incredible wealth in the World to Come. Moreover, the harder we work to do the mitzvah, the greater the benefit to us. Mitzvos connect us to Hashem. They are His directions to us on how to live and how to feed and care for our *neshamah*.

With all this in mind, we can see that we assert a very poor argument when we pray for Hashem to help us in return for the mitzvos we've done. Rashi (*Devarim* 3:23) quotes Chazal's advice that we should consider anything Hashem does for us as a "free gift," which we have done nothing to earn. All these ideas can be summed up in two words: humble heart. That is what we have to bring to Hashem when we pray. It has to be real, coming from sincere gratitude for everything He does for us and sincere understanding of how greatly we benefit from what we do for Him. When we pray with a humble heart, our prayers stir Hashem's love and care, and they are answered.

A True Story

A young girl in Eretz Yisrael walked into a jewelry store and pointed out a beautiful gold bracelet to the owner. "I'd like to buy this, please," she said. The owner watched in disbelief as the girl pulled coins out of her pocket to pay for her purchase. They added up to seven shekalim and eight agurot — about $2.30.

"I'm sorry," said the owner to the girl, "but this bracelet costs 3,000 shekalim. You need much more money to buy it. Who is it for?"

"I want to buy it for my older sister," the girl explained.

"You see, my mother died a few years ago, and ever since then, my sister has been taking care of us. She really tries to do everything Mommy used to do. She cooks and cleans the house and even does my homework with me. Today is her 18th birthday and we're making her a little party. I wanted to buy her a nice gift to show her how much we appreciate what she does."

The storeowner was touched. He gift-wrapped the bracelet and told the girl, "You have just the right amount of money for this." That night, beaming with excitement, the children gave their sister the gift. When she opened the box and saw the gold bracelet gleaming against the velvet lining, she knew her siblings could never have afforded it.

The next day, she went to the store and asked the owner how much her sister had paid for the bracelet. "Seven shekalim and eight agurot," he said. "Sometimes mending a broken heart is worth much more than gold."

MAKE IT REAL:

Before you pray for something you want or need, think of a few precious gifts you already have and realize that they are yours only because of Hashem's kindness.

3

When You Don't Know What to Say

Did someone's words ever give you the boost to keep going?

Tova's parents were getting divorced. Tova tried hard to keep her spirits up by focusing on her *emunah* that Hashem would make everything work out in the best way possible. Of all Tova's friends, only her closest friend, Kayla, knew about the situation. For Kayla, this position was both an honor and a burden. On one hand, Tova had chosen her as the one friend in whom she was allowed to confide, since her family did not want the news to spread. On the other hand, Kayla felt a heavy responsibility for finding the right words to give Tova encouragement, while still keeping their friendship as normal and happy as it had always been.

In a situation like this, in which our words are so important, we may worry that we'll say the wrong thing. We might even avoid the person to avoid the awkwardness, or talk about everything except for the massive, monster challenge looming over our friend's shoulder.

When our words really count — which they always do! — we can ask Hashem to send us the right words to say. Before we begin *Shemoneh Esrei,* we recognize that our ability to use our speech for good purposes is nothing other than a gift from Hashem. We say, "Hashem, open my lips that my mouth will declare Your praise," reminding ourselves that even the praise we give Hashem comes from Hashem.

When our intentions are good and we turn to Hashem for the right words, we can accomplish miracles with our power of speech. You know this first-hand because we've all experienced these miracles: Did someone's words ever stir up a great idea in your head? Did someone's encouragement ever give you a boost of power to keep going when your motivation was low? Did someone's comforting words ever help you get over pain or disappointment? Did someone ever teach you something that improved your *davening* or inspired you to do a mitzvah? Did someone ever explain something to you in a way that suddenly made it clear?

As this true story related by Dr. Weiss proves, the right words can even save a life:

> *Aaron's father was in the hospital. Although he had a serious illness, his immediate challenge was that he had lost his interest in living. He wouldn't eat or get out of bed. He seemed to just be waiting for the end to come. Aaron and his brothers and sisters were all staying by their father's bedside, worried that he might leave them at any moment.*
>
> *Aaron decided to call Dr. Weiss and ask him to come to the hospital to visit his father. Although Dr. Weiss wasn't treating his father, Aaron thought that maybe his position as a doctor would give his words the power to break through the patient's hopeless mood. Dr. Weiss agreed to come, but he had no idea what he could possibly say. If he couldn't offer a cure for the man's illness, what could he tell him that would make him feel better?*
>
> *Dr. Weiss prayed on the way to the hospital, "Please, Hashem, give me the right words to say to give this man strength." When he arrived at the patient's room, he still did not know what he was going to say. There was no inspiring speech running through his mind. However, he began to speak, and he himself was surprised by the words that came out of his mouth. He felt certain that Hashem had sent them to him.*
>
> *"All your life, you've taught your children how to live and how to serve Hashem," the doctor told the patient.*

"You are still their teacher. Now you have to teach them how a Jew faces sickness. You have to find your strength and show them how Hashem wants us to serve Him even during hard times."

The words not only penetrated the patient's heart but inspired the children as well. The next day, one of the family members called Dr. Weiss to tell him great news. The father's strength was coming back. He was eating and he had even gone for a walk!

Our words can accomplish so much, often in a few brief minutes. We can add days or even years to a person's life. We can help someone return to Torah. We can give someone the idea that turns into his successful business or *chesed*. We can help someone understand his math. But we can only do this because Hashem gives us the power of speech and in His kindness, He gives us the right words at the right time. It's a gift we must treasure and protect by never misusing it.

MAKE IT REAL:

Discover the power of your speech by saying something positive to one person — a friend or family member — each day. If you choose someone with whom your relationship is a bit challenging, you'll see even more noticeable results. And be sure to ask Hashem to give you the right words first.

4

You Made the Right Choice

Don't worry. It turned out perfectly.

Some people have a hard time making choices. They worry about making a mistake. What if things don't work out as they are hoping? What if the other choice would be better? Often, even after a person makes his choice, he still worries and wonders if he would have been more successful had he taken the other path. Most difficult of all is when a person runs into trouble because of the choice he made. Then he's full of regret. He believes that he listened to the wrong advice or didn't look into the situation well enough. Had he approached the matter differently, everything would be fine. Instead, he's suffering.

In reality, we have no reason to be wrapped up in indecision, or to kick ourselves due to what we regard as a poor choice. That is because we do not make the choices. Hashem directs us along the path He has chosen for us. He tells us whether to turn right or left. We have a *hishtadlus* to do, which is to gather as much information as we can and consult wiser people when we need advice. Then we must make a decision — the best one we can make with the information we have available to us.

Even if later we discover that there is something we did not know, and that this information would have led us to decide differently, we have no cause for regret. We didn't make a mistake. Rather, Hashem kept that information from us because He wanted us to take the path that we chose.

For example, a girl who is graduating high school needs to choose a seminary for the coming year. Unsure of whether she wants to go to Eretz Yisrael or stay closer to home, she applies to both and receives acceptance letters from two seminaries — one in a city near her home and the other 6,000 miles away. She speaks to girls who have gone to each of the seminaries she is considering. She discusses the matter with her parents and her advisor at school.

For three weeks, her thoughts toss back and forth between the two options. She can imagine herself homesick and lonely far away, but she can also imagine herself feeling that she's missing out on a once-in-a-lifetime experience if she stays local. Finally, she decides to go to Eretz Yisrael. Everyone has warned her that the first few months might be difficult. However, she thinks, "This isn't just difficult. This is unbearable! Why did I do this to myself?" The unfamiliar surroundings, the rapid-fire Hebrew being spoken everywhere, the Shabbos meals with strange families, and her longing for family and friends made her want nothing more than to curl up in her own bed in her own room. It all added up to one word in her mind: MISTAKE. "Had I realized what this was going to be like, I never would have done it!" she thinks. "Why didn't I listen to my friends who warned me that I wasn't the type for Eretz Yisrael?"

We could well understand why this girl believes she made a mistake. However, she could begin to alleviate her suffering by dropping this idea and telling herself instead, "Hashem sent me here. He didn't do it to hurt me, but to help me. It's not what I thought it would be, but I will try to make the most of it." Regret not only stops us from moving forward with optimism and energy, but also feeds a false idea: that things could be different. This is simply not so, because our choice was in Hashem's hands and we are experiencing exactly what He wants us to experience.

Sometimes choices have a dire result: a person decides to attend a *simchah* on a snowy night and is injured in a car accident on the way. He thinks, "If only I had stayed home." Sometimes choices have a wonderful result: a man decides to sell a certain product in his store and it becomes incredibly popular. He thinks, "What a smart business decision I made!" But in neither case is the person responsible for the outcome of his decision. He is only responsible for the *hishtadlus* that goes into making the decision.

In one area, however, we are fully responsible for our choices. "Everything is determined by Hashem except for *yiras Shamayim,*" the Gemara (*Berachos* 33b) states. When we must decide whether to serve Hashem or follow our base desires, Hashem does not direct our decision. We make that choice and we can choose wrong. In that case, regret is exactly the right response. It leads us to *teshuvah* and erases our sin. At that point, regret has no more purpose because the sin no longer exists. In fact, when a sin leads us to do *teshuvah* out of love, regretting that we violated the words of Hashem, our great and beloved Father, the sin is now counted as a mitzvah!

In all other situations, we can take so much stress out of our lives by understanding the limits of our power to choose. We need not lie in bed at night constantly re-running the pros and cons of a decision. Neither do we need to worry that we will come to regret our decision. If we've gathered all the information available to us at the time, given the matter thought and sought out advice, we can confidently make a move. It will be exactly what Hashem wanted.

MAKE IT REAL:

The next time you find yourself unable to decide after thoughtfully considering your options, tell yourself, "Whatever I decide will be the right decision."

5

You Can't Lose

Choosing what Hashem wants is always the right choice.

Only human beings face choices. Animals follow their instincts, but people must always weigh their instincts against their sense of right and wrong. Jews must go even further, weighing everything against the values that the Torah teaches us — and this can be a very tricky business.

That's because the *yetzer hara* has an impressive set of ploys that it uses to sway our decision. It doesn't just sit on our shoulder like a little cartoon devil, whispering "Do a bad thing," in our ear. It knows we don't want to do a bad thing. Instead, it disguises itself as a wise, logical friend who says, "Do the smart thing." Or it might be a fun-loving friend who says, "You have to loosen up!" Or it might be the practical friend who says, "You'll never pass the test if you don't cheat a little. Everyone does." In all these instances, we think that somehow, our own benefit is on one side of the scale and Hashem's will is on the other. Since we know Hashem loves us and that He understands our weaknesses, we might fall for the *yetzer hara's* strategy. Does Hashem really expect any more from us?

Devarim Rabbah (2:5) says that He does. Hashem tells us in the simplest, most direct way how to make a choice: "Listen to Me, because no one ever loses by listening to Me." Even if an option that contradicts the Torah seems more logical, more exciting, more practical or more realistic, we will not gain from it. At first, the right choice might seem to bring the wrong result, but the words of the *Midrash* assure us that ultimately, we will come out the winner.

That doesn't make the right choice easy. Sticking to our standards can put us in the middle of many dramatic moments. Imagine a girl named Sarah standing with a group of friends at recess. She isn't the most confident, popular girl in the group; she tries hard to fit in. One of the girls begins speaking *lashon hara* about a classmate, and Sarah is well aware of how destructive this is. She knows she should either try to move the conversation onto another track or walk away from it. But will she? Does Hashem really expect her to be the one to take a stand when she's trying so hard just to have friends? We can almost hear the competing voices battling it out in her head as she stands there. But if she can see the *Midrash* in bright, bold letters before her eyes, she'll have the confidence to do what is right. In the following true story about the musician Alex Clare, we see how Hashem comes through for someone who chooses His will even when fame and fortune are at stake:

> *Alex was born in 1985 in London. With musical talent that became obvious at a young age, he began playing instruments, singing and composing songs professionally. When he was 22, he started learning about Torah and was moved by what he learned. His first commitment was eating kosher; then he began to keep Shabbos.*
>
> *Meanwhile, a major record company wanted him to sign a contract. He agreed on the condition that he would not be asked to perform on Shabbos. Although musicians need to perform at concerts to promote their albums, and concerts are often scheduled for Friday nights, the record company agreed to Alex's condition.*
>
> *Alex recorded his first album. Every opportunity he was offered to appear in concert was on a Friday night, and he turned them all down. Then a great opportunity to tour with a famous singer came up. "It's Passover," Alex explained to the record producer. "I can't perform." When an even better opportunity arose — scheduled for Succos — Alex rallied his courage and said "no." The*

company threatened to cancel his contract. How could they sell his records if he wouldn't promote them?

At that time, Alex was nearly penniless, yet he was turning down a fortune. He began to think about the words of "Unesaneh Tokef," the Yom Kippur piyyut written by Rabbi Amnon, who gave up his life for Torah. Was a record contract such a big sacrifice? He gave the record company his final answer; he would not perform. Not only did he lose his contract, but also his reputation in the industry. In need of encouragement, he went to see Rabbi Dovid Tugendhaft, his Rabbi. "Is losing everything my reward for keeping the mitzvos?" he asked.

The Rabbi comforted him with this thought: Avraham Avinu spent his whole life teaching the world about a loving, kind G-d. Suddenly when already elderly, he was commanded to offer his own son as a sacrifice, turning everything he stood for on its head. However, he listened to Hashem and he lost nothing. Instead, this episode became one of the greatest moments in history.

The next few months were difficult for Alex. Then one day, Microsoft called and asked to use one of his songs for an ad for a new product. Soon, the song became a top hit in Europe and the U.S. and his album sold six million copies. Alex had held on tight during a few rough years, but in the end, he did not lose by choosing Hashem.

MAKE IT REAL:

Imagine a poster, a banner, a sign written in neon lights that says, "Listen to Me, because no one ever loses by listening to Me," and call it to mind when you have a difficult choice to make.

6

There Is No "Should Be"

When we hold back our frustration, we are passing the test.

Does it ever seem that Hashem is "picking on you"? One thing after another goes wrong, and then comes the final straw that makes you say, "Now *this* has to happen?" At times like this, we tend to feel that things are not as they "should be."

> *Your morning gets off to a rough start. You oversleep and now you're rushed. You can't find your left shoe, and by the time you find it, there are only three minutes left for breakfast. In your hurry to eat, you knock over your orange juice. Do you have time to clean it up? Well, you can't just leave it there, so you grab some paper towels and swish them around, run out to the bus stop and arrive just as the bus is pulling away.*
>
> *Now you're furious. Nothing went according to plan, and now you're left having to find a ride to school. You stomp back home in a miserable mood. You might end up coming late, which will mean even more trouble.*

If events like this make you furious, you will find yourself being furious very often, because many times, things don't go exactly the way we plan. Do you have another choice?

Emunah gives you another, much better choice. Our frustration grows from the feeling that what has happened isn't fair; it isn't as it should be. In our minds, we're kicking and screaming like a toddler whose Mommy won't give him the cookie he wants. Our desires might be a lot more meaningful than a cookie — getting to school on time is certainly important — but our approach is no more mature or refined.

With *emunah* in Hashem, we understand that the events we experience are exactly as they should be. The fact that they are not to our liking is actually Hashem's gift to us — an opportunity to accept the circumstances as His will and to make the best of them. When we hold back our impatience and frustration and say, "OK, I'll just do what I can," then we are passing the test with flying colors, recognizing that Hashem runs the world, and we are taking a step toward fulfilling our purpose in the world.

> *You run outside and see the bus pulling away. "I guess Hashem didn't want me on that bus today," you think. Calmly, you look around, thinking about what to do next. You notice your neighbor heading off to work. "Could you give me a lift to school? I missed my bus," you explain. "Sure. Hop in!" he replies. You arrive before the bus.*

By keeping anger and frustration out of the picture, we pass the test that *Tehillim* (11:5) tells us to expect with the words "Hashem tests the righteous." This means that when we feel He is picking on us, the truth is just the opposite. He sees us as ready and able to pass the test. Each time we step back and let go of what we think "should be," we take another step up the ladder to greatness. And we live a calmer, happier life!

REALITY CHECK:

Try it! The next time you feel frustration boiling up inside you, stop and tell yourself, "This is my test. I'm going to pass it!"

7

It's All Avodas Hashem

In every time, place, and situation, we can serve Hashem.

Right now, as this book is being written, the world is still in the midst of the Covid-19 pandemic. *Baruch Hashem,* we are not experiencing the same level of sickness and death we experienced when the illness first hit in March, 2020. However, we can all remember those days and how strange our world became: no *minyanim,* no yeshivah, tiny backyard weddings, Pesach *Sedarim* without guests. If anyone would have suggested in January, 2020, that this is how the world would look two months later, he would have been thought crazy.

With so many roads blocked in our *avodas Hashem,* many people felt miserable and depressed. How could learning Torah on a conference call or Zoom compare to learning with a *chavrusa* in a bustling *beis medrash*? How could *davening* in the dining room compare with *davening* with a *minyan?* How could a grandfather teach the next generation about *yetzias Mitzrayim* when he and his wife sat alone at their Seder?

We all bemoaned what we were missing. Even now, our *avodas Hashem* seems to be running along at half-speed. Yeshivos are continually opening and closing as new cases of Covid are diagnosed. Shuls struggle with rules about masks and social distancing. *Simchos* are overshadowed by the need to prevent Covid's spread; relatives who would normally run to share our *simchos* now stay away.

"What is going on?" we wonder. "Doesn't Hashem want our *avodah*? Doesn't He want us to be in school, in yeshivah, learning Torah? Doesn't He want us to come together to pray and to share each other's *simchos*? Doesn't He want guests at our table?"

Rather than feeling confused and depressed by the situation, we can find encouragement in the knowledge that our *avodah* is not being rejected at all. Rather, Hashem is giving us a different *avodah*. That is to serve Him to the best of our ability in the situation He has created. We saw and continue to see an incredible outpouring of creative ideas that enable learning, *tefillah, simchos,* and mitzvos to continue. One example is the "drive-by" *vort*. Another is the porch *minyan*. Still another is the virtual fundraising dinner. And there are dozens, if not hundreds, of other examples. Even those who, for health reasons, have no option but to stay quarantined in their homes are fulfilling Hashem's will in doing so. Whenever we accept the situation Hashem has handed us and serve Him from there in the best way possible, our *avodah* is perfect.

> *The Noam Elimelech and his brother Reb Zusha were traveling together when an anti-Semitic officer stopped them, questioned them and, dissatisfied with their answers, threw them in jail. As they sat in their tiny, dingy cell, Reb Zusha looked miserable. "Where is your emunah?" his brother asked.*
>
> *"I'm not down about being in jail," Reb Zusha replied. "I'm sad that we will not be able to daven Minchah in here." He pointed to a bucket in the corner in which the prisoners relieved themselves. Praying with such an item in the room was clearly not permitted.*
>
> *"But Who commanded us to daven Minchah?" Rabbi Elimelech asked. "Hashem! And Who forbade us to pray under these conditions? Hashem! What does it matter which mitzvah we are doing as long as it's the will of Hashem? Right now, by not davening, we're serving Him!"*
>
> *Reb Zusha became so elated by this new perspective*

that he rose and began dancing. His brother joined him and soon, the two tzaddikim were dancing joyfully around the pail, happy to be fulfilling Hashem's will.

Determined to put an end to the prisoner's joy, the guard rushed in and removed the pail. The brothers instantly began to daven a long, heartfelt Minchah and soon after that, they were released.

Rabbi Elimelech explained the entire strange series of events quite simply: "We fulfilled Hashem's will by not praying, and then Hashem enabled us to pray. In the merit of both, we were released from prison."

Regardless of the situation in which we find ourselves, when we realize that we are living the life Hashem wants us to be living at that moment, we bring His blessing.

MAKE IT REAL:

Whether Covid or some other life situation is standing in the way of your sincere effort to serve Hashem, choose to do your best under the circumstances and take heart in the fact that in Hashem's eyes, your avodah is perfect.

8

Pray All the Way

In Hashem's world, nothing is more likely or less likely.

When we pray, the *emunah* that we hold inside us has a chance to come out into the world. In a way, it's like creating a painting of an image we have in our head. What does our *emunah* look like? The feelings and thoughts we have while we pray paint the picture.

One important feature of *emunah* is that Hashem has no limits. He can do anything at all at any time. Nothing is "too much" for Him and it's never too late for Him to turn a situation around. But do our prayers express this idea? Do we really feel it in our heart and believe that He can answer any prayer — even for something that might seem impossible?

Sometimes our prayers, if we tune in to ourselves, show that we do not firmly believe Hashem can grant us anything we need. We might face a huge challenge, but instead of asking Hashem to fix the whole situation in the best possible way, we ask Him for something we think is more likely to happen.

> *Yoni is in the middle of 12th grade, and like his friends, he's busy applying to beis medrash for the coming year. He's been preparing with a tutor for months, trying to make up for the fact that he has never been a strong learner. Tomorrow is his interview, which includes an oral test on Gemara, at the yeshivah he really wants to attend. He prays, "Hashem, please let me get in! I don't*

need to sound like a genius, just don't let me make a fool of myself!"

Yoni thinks that by asking for something that seems more likely for a poor student to achieve, his prayers are more likely to be answered. In his mind, praying to perform at a high level and answer every question with confidence is asking for "the impossible." This reveals a hole in his *emunah*, because in Hashem's world, nothing is more likely or less likely; everything is exactly as Hashem decides it should be, no matter what the "chances."

When we pray for important matters, we can and we should pray for the very best outcome. If we're praying for someone who is very sick, we shouldn't just ask Hashem to let him survive, but rather, to bring him back to his full health and strength. If we're praying for someone who is poor, we shouldn't say, "Please let him have enough to support his family," but instead, "Let him become rich!"

Certainly in our growth in Torah and mitzvos, we should "go for it" and pray to become *talmidei chachamim* and *tzaddikim*. There is nothing selfish or unrealistic about asking Hashem to give us everything we and others need in its full measure. In fact, it's just the opposite. These kinds of prayers paint a picture of an *emunah* that is bright and detailed and complete.

MAKE IT REAL:

Think about your prayers. Have you been holding back on asking for things you consider "impossible"? Take one area that would help you grow and achieve more in your life, and ask Hashem for the best possible outcome.

9

Only Hashem Knows When

Trusting Hashem means trusting His timing.

"If someone told me that two years from now, I'd be married, I would just relax and take advantage of my time being single," said Malka, a 23-year-old girl who was hoping and praying for a shidduch.

"If I knew when I will finally get a job, I would feel so much calmer when I get turned down," said an unemployed father.

"If I knew that in the end, I'll get into seminary, I wouldn't worry about all these interviews," said a girl who dreamed of learning for a year in Eretz Yisrael.

"If I could be sure that all this review will actually help me become a top student, I wouldn't mind the struggle," said a boy for whom learning had always been difficult.

One of the hardest parts of keeping *emunah* strong is trusting that everything will work out for us in the end, even when at the moment, we're struggling. Most people can get through a difficult challenge if they see their goal in sight. It's like running a race; you can run your hardest to get to the finish line because your motivation is high and your energy is revved up to win. But if you're not quite sure there *is* a finish line, how can you stay motivated? In your mind, you're thinking, "I can't keep going like this forever!" You slow down and eventually give up.

To build strong *emunah* that will take us through tough times in life, we have to not only trust Hashem, but trust His timing. So much of our worry comes from our need to see the goal and keep it in clear sight. Only then do we trust that our struggle is leading to a positive ending. We think, "I can keep going for another mile."

With real trust in Hashem, we don't have to see the ending in order to stay calm and positive. We know without a doubt that He is taking us where we need to go, to the place that is best for us. We know that our struggles are just tests that make us stronger. Our effort is never wasted. Instead of thinking that "maybe it's never going to happen," we think, "something good will come out of this if I just hold on to Hashem." If we face our challenges with this outlook, we will see that our answer will come at the right time in the right way. With *emunah*, we really *can* see all the way to the finish line, because we trust that wherever we find ourselves in life, we are heading to the good things Hashem has in store for us.

A TRUE STORY

Frieda, Chana, and Menucha Klein were three sisters, all of marriageable age and all single. Frieda was already 27. Years of tefillah and tears had flowed, but as time went on, Frieda remained single and her sisters joined the "waiting line." Finally, the Kleins decided to travel to Eretz Yisrael, daven at the Kosel, and seek berachos from Gedolim.

On the last day of the trip, the father received a phone call from his friend back in Brooklyn. The friend told Mr. Klein that when his own daughters were in shidduchim, he paid for the wedding of a poor kallah, and in each case, the daughter was soon married. Now, he said, someone was calling him from Bnei Brak trying to raise money for a poor widow, a Bais Yaakov teacher, whose daughter was getting married.

Mr. Klein was no millionaire — paying for another girl's wedding was not easy for him. However, he decided to do it. He and his family rushed to Bnei Brak before they had to leave for America, met the widow, and gave her a check. She cried tears of joy as she hugged Mrs. Klein and promised that her students would daven for the three Klein girls.

Four months later, Menucha, the youngest sister, was engaged. Her chassan's cousin thought of the perfect match for her sister Chana; it was a boy who had lived right across the street from the Kleins for the past 20 years. Chana's father-in-law then thought of a match for Frieda — a boy three years younger than her, who had been living down the block his entire life.

When Hashem decided that the time was right, He revealed solutions that had been there all along. This can happen to anyone. We need to stop telling ourselves "It isn't happening" and instead, keep praying and crying to Hashem, because all we really know is that "it hasn't happened yet."

MAKE IT REAL:

Can you recall something you thought would never happen, but finally it did? Remind yourself of that situation when you find yourself thinking that your prayers are not being answered.

10

But This Is Different!

The circumstances may change but Hashem does not.

Betzalel landed in Tel Aviv. It was finally real! He had come to Eretz Yisrael to study in yeshivah. For a number of reasons, he had left his old yeshivah in New York a bit earlier than his friends. He had talked it over with his Rosh Yeshivah and his parents, and they agreed that this would be the best plan for him. He was apprehensive about going to Eretz Yisrael on his own, but friendly, sociable Betzalel reassured himself that he wouldn't be alone for long.

Now, standing in the middle of Ben Gurion Airport, he suddenly felt a wave of anxiety rise up in him. Which way should he go? As he followed the crowd to the baggage claim area, worries began to pop up in his mind — pop, pop, pop, one after another in quick succession, like popcorn on a stove. What if he got lost? What if his cab driver was actually a terrorist? What if he couldn't stand his roommates? What if they couldn't stand him? What if he got sick so far from home? What if he couldn't find a good chavrusa?

Why did all these worries suddenly crowd Betzalel's mind? It was because he found himself in a new place and suddenly, the support system he was accustomed to — his friends, family, and yeshivah, his own house and familiar hometown — were gone. He felt like a cartoon character who steps off a cliff, looks down, and suddenly realizes that there's nothing holding him up.

In reality, though, none of the supports he had relied upon back home had ever been holding him up; he was in Hashem's hands the whole time, and he still was. Hashem had not let him fall up until this point. The fact that he found himself in new surroundings didn't change anything. The same Hashem Who took care of him in New York would take care of him in Yerushalayim. In fact, if Betzalel needed more help because he was living away from home, Hashem would take even better and closer care of him than He did before.

This fact — that our protection comes from Hashem and not from our circumstances — was one of the lessons the Jewish people learned from the *mahn* that Hashem fed them in the Wilderness. Torah commentators (*Rashbam, Ibn Ezra*) explain that the test of the *mahn* was that each family received only what they needed for that day. Even if they wanted to put some aside for tomorrow, they could not, because anything left overnight would spoil. That means that every night, they went to bed with an "empty fridge." This taught them that they need only rely on Hashem for the food that kept them alive.

What seems strange about this test is that it continued for 40 years. We would think that after a few years, they would have complete trust in Hashem's care. After all, if He took care of them yesterday and the day before that, for years on end, how could they still doubt Him?

The answer is clear from Betzalel's worries, and from many of our worries as well. If Hashem has taken care of our needs up until this moment, if He's put a roof over our head, food on our table, and loving, caring people in our lives, why don't we trust Him yet?

It's because we think, "This is different." We imagine that Hashem was "capable" of taking care of us before, but now something has happened that changes matters. Nothing changes for Hashem! No matter where we are, no matter what we're going through, He is still there, handing us the exact portion of *berachah* we need to fulfill the purpose of each day.

MAKE IT REAL:

When you find yourself worrying, ask yourself, "Hasn't Hashem taken care of me every day until now?"

11

What's the Use in Trying?

The greater the effort, the greater the reward.

"I'm trying to do what Hashem wants. Why does He make it so difficult for me?"

You try to raise money for a poor *kallah* and end up with a few hundred dollars.

You want to become a *talmid chacham* but the Gemara leaves you bored and confused.

You worked hard so you could get into a high-level yeshivah but you are rejected.

You try to concentrate on your *davening* but random thoughts keep popping into your head.

You try to help your mother by cooking dinner for the family and it comes out inedible.

In all these cases, a person might throw up his or her hands and say, "I guess there's no point in trying. Hashem obviously doesn't want me to succeed."

If that is what we think, however, we are getting the wrong message. Success is not the point of trying to do a mitzvah; the point of trying is trying. Trying hard, trying our best, doing all we can with the talents, brains, and situation Hashem has given us: This is the measure of a mitzvah. In fact, if we set out to do a mitzvah but something beyond our control stops us from completing it, Hashem still rewards us for it.

Often, when we do try our best and persist even when we encounter obstacles, Hashem ultimately leads us to the success we were seeking. The problem arises when we see these obstacles as a message from Above that says, "It's not meant to be" rather than "Try a little harder." Why is Hashem making it difficult? It is because He wants us to have the merit of the extra effort.

Imagine how Avraham Avinu felt when he sat by his tent under the hot sun, feeling the pain of his *bris milah,* and yet hoping that Hashem would send him guests in need of hospitality. Avraham knew that this mitzvah, which he always performed with such vim and vigor, would be hard for him this time. No one would fault him if he preferred to relax and take care of his health, rather than serving guests, on that particular day.

Avraham never considered that thought because he knew that the greater the effort, the greater the merit of the mitzvah. Chazal (*Bava Metzia* 86b) tell us that this one instance of *hachnassas orchim,* among the hundreds of thousands Avraham performed in his lifetime, provided the merit that protected our nation for 40 years as we journeyed in the Wilderness. In the merit of the food he gave the guests, Hashem provided the *mahn.* The water he gave them earned his children the Well of Miriam. The shade he provided, as he stood over them while they ate, translated into the Clouds of Glory that protected *Bnei Yisrael* from the desert sun. All of this happened because of the supreme effort Avraham exerted in serving his guests when circumstances made it so very difficult for him.

We often see that when we persist, we reach a breakthrough. Even if we do not, the effort is never wasted because Hashem treasures the effort more than we can imagine.

A TRUE STORY

Learning Torah, Levi believed, was the greatest purpose of a Jew's life, and that is why his difficulties in learning were so painful for him. After several years of struggling in beis medrash, he began to believe that Hashem was directing him toward a different path.

One night, as he was about to get into bed after a long, exhausting day, he realized that he had forgotten to pray Maariv. "Oh, no," he thought. "Maybe I'll just pray alone for tonight." But his conscience spoke louder. "Get dressed and go find a minyan." That's just what he did, and he later told a friend that "It was one of the best prayers I ever prayed."

However, that shot of inspiration wasn't enough to prevent him from another, silent "Oh, no," when a person at the minyan asked him for a ride home. Levi just wanted to get back into bed! However, his better nature quickly took over and he agreed to give the man a ride. The two men hit it off and the passenger became Levi's study partner. He was a phenomenal teacher who had the ability to make the Gemara clear as daylight for Levi. Levi's learning took off. Hashem had sent him the answer to his prayers not just because he had prayed Maariv with a minyan, but because he had struggled to overcome his resistance and done what had come hard to him.

MAKE IT REAL:

When you're struggling to do a mitzvah, dig in and keep pushing, knowing that your efforts, whether or not they succeed, are earning you great merit.

12

You Did Such Good Work; Here's More!

No reward is better than a mitzvah.

Imagine that it's the day before Pesach and your mother asks you to scrub the kitchen floor, getting deep into the corners and crevices one last time to make sure that no speck of chametz is left. You have made other plans with friends, but before you try to shift the job onto someone else or put it off for later, you think, "It's Erev Pesach and my mother asked for my help. I'm going to do what I'm supposed to do." An hour and a half later, you're exhausted but satisfied as you look at the floor, which now appears brand-new. Your mother is also thrilled, so thrilled in fact that she "hires" you for the next task on her list. "I need a bunch of boxes brought down from the attic," she says. "Have something to eat and rest a little bit and then you can bring them down for me."

We would not think of a second chore as much of a reward for doing such a great job on the first chore. However, it is a great reward — because it's a chance to do another mitzvah, which means adding another fortune to our account in *Olam Haba*.

Like this mother, Hashem rewards our good work with another chance to serve Him. This is the meaning of *Chazal's* words, "The reward for a mitzvah is a mitzvah." A mitzvah is the best reward Hashem can give us in this world because the real reward — the indescribably wonderful reward He has for us in the Next World — cannot be contained by physical beings in a physical world. For now, it is beyond us. Therefore, when Hashem sees that we want to serve Him, He rewards us with more opportunities to do so. He creates a situation in which one mitzvah leads to another and then another, so that our Heavenly reward continues to mount.

We often see this in our everyday life. For instance, a man picks up a boy who needs a ride home from yeshivah. He discovers that the boy lives on the same block as his elderly uncle, so he decides to stop by and say hello. His uncle, who is in poor health, mentions that he's out of bread and milk, and so the man offers to run out to the grocery store and buy the items for his uncle. One mitzvah leads to the next. This is Hashem's reward, and it is the greatest reward we could ever ask for.

In this true story, we see that incredible accomplishments can result from this process of mitzvah leading to mitzvah:

> *Daniel lived in an apartment building in New York. One day, he was standing outside the building talking to his sisters when a homeless woman asked him for help. Instead of giving her money, he decided to make a real kiddush Hashem and buy her some food. With his kippah on his head, he came out of the nearby store with food in hand and gave it to the woman.*
>
> *There was a hotel next door to Daniel's apartment building, and the doorman of that hotel had witnessed the entire episode. The next day, the doorman saw Daniel and asked him to come into his office. Having noticed Daniel's yarmulke, the doorman thought he might be interested in an item that had been left behind by a guest. It was about to be discarded because of the hotel rule that lost items were kept for only 30 days.*
>
> *"You're Jewish, right?" the doorman said. "Maybe you have a use for this." To Daniel's amazement, it was a bag containing tallis and tefillin. "I would love to have it to return it to the owner," Daniel said. "Can you give me his name?" The doorman was not permitted to give out that information.*
>
> *Examining the bag's contents, Daniel discovered*

a yarmulke inscribed with the date and location of a simchah that took place in France. He called his Rabbi, who was familiar with the French community. From the lettering on the tallis bag, his Rabbi figured out that the person's first name was Yoan, a common name in France, and that his last name began with "ches." With that information, Daniel looked up all the "Yoan Ches" names in France and made a list.

He went to the doorman. "If I tell you the name, will you tell me if he stayed here?" The doorman agreed. Daniel finally identified his man and using an email address that the doorman supplied, he let him know that he had found his tefillin. It turned out that Yoan had just recently moved from France. When Daniel came to deliver the tefillin, the two men hit it off and spoke for four hours. Daniel became Yoan's first American friend.

But that wasn't all. Yoan was just beginning to keep the mitzvos, and Daniel encouraged him to grow. When Daniel discovered that Yoan and his wife had only had a secular wedding in France, he organized a Jewish wedding for them. During the following three years, the couple became completely observant.

It all started with Daniel's flash of inspiration to make a *kiddush Hashem* by feeding the homeless woman. From there, Hashem served up one opportunity after until, giving Daniel the chance to take an active hand in bringing an entire family closer to Torah and mitzvos.

MAKE IT REAL:

Grab that mitzvah! Recognize when the opportunity is in front of you that it's Hashem, trying to give you His most lavish reward.

13

Everything's Under Control

We never have to do it alone.

Imagine you are in the worst predicament of your life. You're so worried and upset that all you can do is sit on the couch and think of all your troubles. Not only are you facing a major challenge, but also, you are obsessed with the dozens of other problems that this challenge might cause.

Suddenly, the door opens and in walks your wise and fabulously wealthy uncle. "Don't worry. Just relax," he tells you. "I'll take care of everything. It's all under control."

What an immense sense of relief you would feel! You know that this uncle has every connection and every resource you could possibly need. He's also experienced, brilliant, and clear-headed. You can be assured that anything he advises you to do will be the right move. Whatever help you need, he can provide.

This is the feeling of security we can have when we build a strong sense of *emunah* in our heart. We never feel alone in our dilemma, because Hashem is always within reach, waiting for our prayers, ready to give us what we need to triumph over the challenge.

Instead of lying awake at night with our mind bouncing back and forth over a difficult decision, we can trust that Hashem will lead us to the right choice. Instead of pondering "what ifs" that might result in disaster, we can trust Hashem to protect us from the things we fear, and even if our fear materializes, we can trust Him to be there with us, giving us the strength to get through it. "*Imo Anochi b'tzarah* — I'm with him in distress," *Tehillim* (91:15) assures us.

We find that when we instill in ourselves a real sense that Hashem is our partner in life, helping us through every challenge, He shows His hand, as this true story illustrates:

> *Yehudah was engaged to be married. Three weeks before his wedding, he began to doubt his decision. Was his bride really the person he wanted to spend the rest of his life with? What had he gotten himself into? He had a strong urge to break the engagement, but how could he cause so much pain to the young woman he was set to marry? How could he cause such chaos and embarrassment for his family? There wasn't any solid reason to break off the engagement; it just didn't seem right for him anymore.*
>
> *"Hashem, I don't know what to do," he prayed with all his heart. "Please help me make the right decision."*
>
> *Just as he was sitting with these troubling thoughts on his mind, he received a phone call. It was a Rabbi to whom he hadn't spoken in several years. Yehudah assumed it was a "mazal tov call" and he hoped his voice wouldn't reveal his doubts.*
>
> *"I heard you're getting married!" the Rabbi exclaimed. "Mazal tov! I want to tell you that I know the girl and her family, and I cannot tell you how perfect a match I think this is." The Rabbi continued enumerating the girl's fine qualities. "You really found a gem!" he concluded.*
>
> *Yehudah hung up the phone a different man. His nerves were calm, his heart was happy, and most of all, he gratefully realized that Hashem had taken care of his dilemma. He had reached into Yehudah's life and helped him make an important decision. The wedding took place and the couple built a happy home filled with children.*

Whatever help we need in life comes from only one Source. If someone is sick and needs healing, Hashem directs him to the right doctor. If someone is broke and needs a job, Hashem connects him with the right opportunity. If someone is single and needs a *shidduch,* He "splits the sea" to find him/her the right spouse. The more we assure ourselves that He is always there, always on the job, ready to help us with the right solution at the right time, the less we are weighed down with worry. We can wait for the solution to emerge because we know without a doubt that everything is under control.

MAKE IT REAL:

The next time you find yourself lost in worry about a situation, imagine the "uncle" in the mashal above walking through the door and telling you, "It's all under control!"

14

Find the Right Address

Hashem decides who will get what they're seeking.

When you want something from someone else — maybe it's something you really need badly — and that person refuses to give it to you, how can you avoid feeling angry? For example, you are absent from school one day and need to borrow someone's notes, but the person you ask says, "I can't spare them. I'm planning on studying tonight." You offer a few suggestions: "How about if I borrow them now and give them back before you start studying?" "How about if you let me know when you're done studying and I'll get them?" But he just keeps saying, "No, that won't work."

Another similar situation: You're raising money for your yeshivah one Purim. You and your friend are lucky enough to have the richest man in town on your list of people to visit. Since your yeshivah is in desperate need of repairs, you're excited about the prospect of being the ones to bring in a big donation. The man is nice enough; he offers you and your friend some food and enthusiastically praises your Rosh Yeshivah. Then he writes a check for $100 — about one-tenth of what you were hoping for. How can you help but wonder, "What's his problem? He could buy the whole yeshivah if he wanted!"

Emunah teaches us that we're looking at these situations the wrong way. Hashem has what we need, and He knows who should be the one to "hold it for us" until the time comes for us to obtain it. These people are not refusing us; they are just not the right address. The *Chovos HaLevavos* writes (in *Shaar HaBitachon*): "A person cannot cause harm or bring benefit to his fellow, or infringe upon what is intended for his fellow, without Hashem's decree."

If our glasses are missing and we looked for them in a pocket and didn't find them there, we wouldn't think of getting angry at the pocket. It simply doesn't have what we're seeking. We only have to know that it's somewhere, and if we keep looking, we'll find it. *Emunah* helps us see disappointment and rejection in the right light: No one can keep something from us that Hashem wants us to have, so when one person says "no," our task is to say "Thanks, anyway" and try elsewhere.

> *"I have the greatest idea," Naomi said to her friend Rochel. "Instead of going to camp this summer, let's make a camp. If we do that and then save our babysitting money next year, we'll both have plenty to pay our expenses in seminary." Both girls were hoping to spend their post-high-school year in Eretz Yisrael, but in both homes, their parents had said they would have to contribute to the costs.*
>
> *"I don't know," Rochel answered. "It's a hassle. You have to advertise and set up and buy a lot of toys and sit outside in the hot sun with a bunch of three-year-olds."*
>
> *Naomi was insistent. "So what? It's worth the effort if it makes us the money we need to go to Eretz Yisrael." Rochel's expression was still negative and she was shaking her head "no" as Naomi spoke. Naomi started to feel angry. Here was her chance, but her best friend — the only person with whom she could imagine making a camp — was too lazy and short-sighted to do it.*

Now is the moment for Naomi's *emunah* to take over. If she gets angry, she is reacting as if Rochel controls whether or not she can go to seminary. If she sees the truth, however, she'll know that Rochel is simply not the channel Hashem has chosen for turning her plan into reality. Someone else might be an even better partner who will help the camp become a greater success, or some other means of earning the money may surface.

MAKE IT REAL:

Practice saying, "He/she doesn't have it for me" when someone refuses something you've requested.

15

Someone Notices You

We all want to feel recognized — and we are.

Imagine you decide to clean up a huge mess in the playroom for your mother. While she's out doing errands, you buckle down and begin picking up toys from the floor, sorting the mess and putting everything away. You grab a giant garbage bag and throw away scribbled papers, crushed pretzels, and a wide variety of other trash your little siblings have left around. When you're three-quarters finished, your brother notices what you're doing and offers to help. While you're taking the garbage bag outside, your mother comes home to find your brother sweeping the floor of a spotless playroom.

"Wow! You're such a *tzaddik*! I can't believe how thoughtful you are to do all this!" she enthuses. You walk in just in time to hear your brother soaking up the praise. It would seem lame at this point to say, "Mom, I did almost all the work and it was my idea." So you just let your good deed go unnoticed.

Everyone wants to feel that his efforts are recognized and rewarded. But as we get older, more and more of what we do is between ourselves and Hashem. Nobody is going to give us a gold star for feeling close to Him when we *daven,* or for overcoming a little bit of annoyance and holding our temper when someone irritates us. People notice when we don't fulfill our responsibilities, but often, they do not notice when we do fulfill them.

The cure to this feeling that "no one notices" is to build up our *emunah,* which assures us that Someone is ALWAYS watching everything we do. Not only does Hashem see our actions, but He hears our inner thoughts as well. When we pray from our hearts, do *chesed* graciously, learn with real enthusiasm and interest, Hashem sees, cares, and will not fail to reward us. In the story below, told by Rabbi Nachman Seltzer, we have a perfect illustration of what this means:

A Rebbetzin called a woman named Batsheva to suggest a shidduch for her son. The girl, named Suri, came highly recommended. She was mature, had wonderful middos, and came from a very well-respected family.

"Sounds perfect!" Batsheva said.

"I do need to tell you, though, that she has a scar on her face. It's pretty obvious, but it doesn't get in her way."

"I'm sorry, Rebbetzin," said Batsheva, "but I don't think that would be for my son."

"I understand," said the Rebbetzin. "But could you just do me one favor? She will be at a wedding tonight and I would just like you to see her for yourself before you say no."

Batsheva did as the Rebbetzin asked. At the wedding, she asked someone to point Suri out to her. She was dancing happily in a circle of friends. Then she broke away and went over to a table where a girl about her age was sitting. The girl was quite overweight and seemed to be reluctant to join the circle. Suri sat and spoke to her for a few minutes, a beautiful smile on her face. Then she stood up, held out her hands, and waited for the girl to grab on. The two girls went into the circle and danced together.

Batsheva was awed by Suri's joyous presence and incredible empathy for her sidelined friend. She didn't even notice the girl's scar.

Two months later, Suri and Batsheva's son were engaged. Suri didn't know it, but her kindness was being watched, and it was abundantly rewarded.

MAKE IT REAL:

When you feel that you're not getting your due recognition, remind yourself that every move you make is being noticed, and every mitzvah you do is rewarded.

16

Pray It With Feeling

The power is in the emotion.

- "I prayed at the Kosel for 40 days and my prayer was answered!"
- "I was so worried about getting into seminary. I *davened* like crazy from the minute we sent in my application. And you know what? I got two acceptances!"
- "They say that Purim morning is an *eis ratzon* (opportune time) for *davening,* so I got up early, went to an early *minyan,* and *davened* for my grandmother to have a *refuah sheleimah.* And a week later she was out of the hospital!

What gives some prayers that extra turbo-power that seems to bring answers in such a clear way? There are special places, like the Kosel or the *kever* of a *tzaddik,* where our prayers are said to have special power. There are also special times — *eis ratzon* — like Purim morning, or as a baby is crying at his *bris.* There are also other *segulos,* like praying for someone who needs the same thing you do.

While all these places, times, and circumstances do have real power, they are only the engine that gets our prayers farther, faster. We have to turn the key to get that engine going, and that key is our heart.

We learn that our *Imahos* Sarah, Rivka, and Rochel were each childless for many years because Hashem wanted to elicit from them their very deepest and most powerful prayers. Hashem knew that they and *Klal Yisrael* would need the merit of those prayers. In the same way, says Rav Tzadok HaKohen, when Hashem wants to give us a gift, but we have not yet merited it, He may give us worries that cause us to pray hard for the very thing He wants to give us. For example, a father suddenly starts worrying about his son getting married. Hashem might well have given him this feeling because He plans to have the son get married soon, but more prayer is needed for it to happen.

The secret behind all these special times, places, and circumstances for prayer is that they focus our emotions on what we're saying. We feel that "this is my chance" and we give it all we've got. We have a real sense that Hashem is listening. While it is true that our prayers get a boost from a *segulah* or an *eis ratzon,* we can boost all our prayers by thinking about each one of them as "my big chance" and giving it our all. Whether the issue is large or small, Hashem is always listening, and always treasures a heartfelt prayer.

A True Story

An American boy was spending a few years learning Torah in Eretz Yisrael. One day, he went to the Kosel to pray. There he noticed an American teenager wearing a Rangers jersey. The boy appeared to be concentrating hard on his prayers, and when he finished, he slipped a note into a crack between the stones.

The yeshivah boy became overwhelmed with curiosity about what was in the note. He said, "Hashem, please forgive me for this," and he removed the note to read it. Here is the plea the boy brought to his Creator: "Hashem, please tell me the score of the Rangers game last night. The WiFi is down, my phone is broken, and I have no way to find out. Please help me."

The yeshivah boy decided to play a prank. He quickly called a friend and asked him to find out who won the Rangers game. It took only a few moments for him to get the answer. He took off after the Rangers fan, who had already left the Kosel area, and caught up with him. "Hi,

I see you're a Rangers fan," he said. "I thought you'd like to know that they won last night, 3-0."

"Wow!" said the other boy. "Hashem answered me right away!"

When the yeshivah boy went back to the beis medrash, he told his rebbi what happened. "He thought Hashem answered his tefillah!" he laughed.

"Why are you laughing?" his rebbi answered. "Hashem did answer him. Through you!"

No prayer is too much or too little. As long as it's said with all our heart, it's a perfect prayer.

MAKE IT REAL:

Use your imagination to ramp up the emotion behind your prayers. Imagine you are standing in front of the Kosel, or visualize your words flying up to Heaven, or whatever other image helps you feel that you're speaking directly to Hashem.

17

All My Needs

Don't skip ahead to the ending.

Every day in the morning *berachos,* we thank Hashem, "*she'asah li kal tzarchi* — Who has provided my every need." If we believe what we're saying and we say it every morning, why do we sometimes feel that our needs are not being met?

One reason is that we're thinking too far ahead. There are things that haven't happened yet. For today, these issues don't create any problems for us, but if they don't resolve in the future...disaster! If we allow our minds to travel down the road and anticipate all the problems that might crop up as we go along, we give up the calm, secure feeling of "*she'asah li kal tzarchi"* and exchange it for a terrifying heap of "what ifs."

Imagine that instead of thinking like this about the journey of life, we thought like this about a vacation journey — perhaps a road trip to the Rocky Mountains. "What if we have bad weather and every hike is ruined? What if it's too hot and we run out of water? What if we get a flat tire on a deserted stretch of highway?"

How enthusiastic would you be about this big adventure? You'd probably talk yourself out of going at all.

You would be even more foolish to be in the middle of the trip, on a beautiful sunny day, surrounded by spectacular scenery, and instead of taking it all in, you sit and worry. "It's nice now, but I see a few clouds. What if it rains later? What if there's no room for us at the campsite? Did the reservations go through? I don't remember getting a confirmation!"

Your whole trip is a waste of time and effort. You would be just as happy sitting in your living room.

Does Hashem give us what we need each day? He does! He gives us our physical needs and He gives us the emotional strength to take on the challenges that are right in front of us. If we don't feel that His care for us is complete, it may be because He is not giving us the strength today to deal with the issues of tomorrow. When we are focused on future worries, we won't find the resources to stay calm and strong. Hashem hasn't yet given them to us. However, when we focus on the here and now, we see that we're alright. We can do it. We can take the next step, the step right in front of us.

When Shani was 15, she was doing the Shabbos shopping for her family and she noticed many young mothers who were doing the same. Many of them had three, four, or more children in tow. Some of the children sat in the shopping carts, some held on to the sides, some clung onto their mothers' skirts. Some mothers even held a cranky baby in one hand while pushing the cart with the other.

"How am I going to get married?" Shani wondered. "I could never do this!"

She had good reason to wonder, because she didn't have much patience. Even her own little sisters and brothers got on her nerves. But as she got closer to shidduch age, her desire to marry overcame her fear of motherhood. Then, when she got married, her desire for a child overcame her fear of being overwhelmed.

Years later, Shani was shopping with her three small children. One was begging for a bag of chips, another was struggling to get out of the wagon, and the third was asleep in her right arm, leaving her with one hand for everything else. She suddenly remembered the moment when she was 15 and declared that she could never do this. Somehow, each step of the way, Hashem had given her the strength, the strategies, and the support she needed to do what came next.

MAKE IT REAL:

When you feel worried or overwhelmed, take stock of your situation NOW and the resources Hashem has given you for today.

18

You Can Be Sure

Knowing is better than believing.

A rebbi was sitting around a table with his students. He asked them, "Do you believe in Hashem?"

The students were shocked by the question. "Of course we do!" they said. "Every day we say Shema Yisrael, Hashem Elokeinu Hashem Echad!"

"Well," said the rebbi, "I don't believe."

Now the students were truly stunned. The rebbi went on. "Do you believe that we are sitting around this table right now?"

"We don't have to believe that," the students answered. "We see it with our own eyes."

"And that is exactly why I don't need to believe in Hashem," the rebbi concluded. "I see it with my own eyes, as the pasuk (Tehillim 19:2) states, 'The heavens declare the glory of G-d and the firmament tells of His handiwork'" (Darchei Mussar, p. 116).

What made this rebbi so certain of Hashem's existence that it was as if he could see Him with his own eyes? Rav Dessler (*Michtav MeEliyahu,* Vol. I) tells us that everything Hashem created, with its amazing precision and complexity, is shouting at us that there's a Creator.

It's interesting to note that the more science learns about the conditions needed for the universe to exist and for Planet Earth to support life, the more scientists have begun to admit that there is an "intelligent design" to Creation. We might not ever hear them saying "I believe in G-d," but we do hear them saying that it is impossible for so many huge forces to be measured out so precisely just by accident.

In 2014, the *Wall Street Journal* ran an article entitled, "Science Increasingly Makes the Case for G-d." It instantly became the most frequently shared opinion article the newspaper had ever run. In it, the author discussed how atheist scientist Carl Sagan's theory that only two conditions were needed to support life had been completely disproven over time. Now, the author said, more than 200 conditions, each of which must be present in precise measure, are known to be necessary.

But the biggest miracle of all, he wrote, was that the universe exists at all. If the ratio among the four forces of astrophysics were out of balance by even one part in 100,000,000,000,000,000, no star could have formed. For such a balance to have come about by chance, "It would be like tossing a coin and having it come up heads 10 quintillion times in a row," said the author. "The universe is the greatest miracle of all time."

For us as Jews, this scientific knowledge can help us solidify our belief in the Creator. However, our *emunah* is much more, because we're not only concerned about the origins of the world, but also about the way we live our daily life. For that, we need to firm up our belief in Hashem's involvement in everything that takes place in the world He created.

Knowing there's a Creator leads us to know that there's a purpose to Creation, which leads us to know that each of us is part of that purpose.

MAKE IT REAL:

Take a good, long look at the night sky. Imagine how small you are from the distance of the moon, from the nearest visible planet, from a faint star that's many light years away. And yet Hashem zooms into your life and guides you with love.

19

What Do You Tell Yourself?

"I am with him in [his] distress" (Tehillim 91:15).

Let's start with an honest question. Is it really possible to have major challenges in life and *not* be unhappy about them? Isn't it only natural to want to be healthy, wealthy, happy, and loved?

A TRUE STORY

The Maggid of Mezerich became the leader of the chassidim after the Baal Shem Tov's passing. His home was the place where the men who would become the next generation of great Rebbes gathered to learn. These students of the Maggid then spread out across Europe and founded many branches of Chassidus. Among these students was Rav Zushe of Anapoli.

One day, a man came to speak to the Maggid. The man's life was filled with troubles and he felt his faith beginning to fade. "How can I feel that Hashem is doing all this to me for my own good?" he asked the Maggid.

"Go to Reb Zushe of Anapoli and he will give you an answer," the Maggid advised the man.

When the man found Reb Zushe, he instantly thought that he knew why the Maggid had sent him there. "This man's clothes are just rags," he thought when he saw Reb Zushe. "And look at that child he's caring for. He's so sickly! This man must be an expert at living with suffering."

Despite his pitiful situation, Reb Zushe greeted his

guest with a warm smile. There was not a trace of strain on his face.

"I was told to come here to learn how someone who has a troubled life can feel that Hashem is doing what is best for him," the man explained to Reb Zushe.

Reb Zushe looked a bit confused by the question. "I'm sorry," he said, "but I can't help you. You see, I've never had a problem in my life. Hashem is always so good to me."

Was the man's trip to visit Reb Zushe a waste? Not at all, because this is exactly what the Maggid wanted the man to learn. Troubles only shatter our faith when we let them do so. Circumstances might be challenging, difficult, or even painful, but our suffering comes from the story we tell ourselves about those circumstances. People who hold on to their *emunah* in tough times are able to do it because all their lives, they see, appreciate, and find joy in every gift Hashem gives them. They know they are loved.

This is the training we need in order to build *emunah* in Hashem's love — *emunah* that is strong enough to last in a time of challenge. If we have that strength, then we are prepared to accept the fact that whatever is happening is Hashem's will, and to recognize that He provides us with non-stop *chesed* as we make our way through our situation. Someone with this point of view feels Hashem's love, even when there are difficult moments. He believes, "This is what has to be, and Hashem is not abandoning me when I need Him."

In *Tehillim* (91:15) we see that Hashem says, "I'm with him in distress." Dovid HaMelech doesn't say there won't be troubles — because sometimes Hashem's plan necessitates that there be hard times — but rather, that in our moment of need, Hashem is there with us. That's our comfort.

MAKE IT REAL:

Write down something you see as a problem in your life. Next to it, in a separate column, list the positive things that are included in or have resulted from that problem. For instance, are there people who have helped you? Lessons you've learned? Have you been able to help others because of your experience?

20

Do We See What They See?

Everyone can see that Hashem loves us.

Did anyone ever tell you something nice about your parents or siblings, and you realize that it's something you never even noticed? For instance, a friend comes to your house for Shabbos for the first time. Later, he tells you, "Your brother is such a nice guy. He really tried to include me in the conversation at the table." You've known your brother all your life, but you never realized that he had this sensitivity to others.

In a similar way, sometimes it takes non-Jews to point out to us what we could have and should have known all along — that we are Hashem's chosen people and that He takes special care of us. In fact, the special status of the Jewish people is Hashem's proof to the rest of the nations that He runs the world.

Tehillim (117:1,2) says, "Praise Hashem, all nations; exalt Him, all the states, for His kindness has overwhelmed us, and the truth of G-d is eternal." This teaches us that when the other nations recognize Hashem's care for His people, they will recognize that He is the one true G-d.

There are so many ways in which our status as the chosen people shows itself. The Jewish people's ability to survive thousands of years in exile is a key proof: Although we've always been few in number, and we've been the subject of numerous decrees and exiles, we're still here. In fact, we are growing and thriving, learning Torah and serving Hashem in historic numbers. In addition, Jews have always created functioning, supportive communities. With Hashem's help, we have organizations that cater to sick children, childless couples, children at risk, people in need of medical or mental health advice, and so much more.

We might not see Hashem's hand in all this, but like the guest at the Shabbos table in the opening scenario, those around us do see it. When the Jewish people act with arrogance, our status makes them angry and spiteful. However, when we act with dignity and are true to our identity as Hashem's people, they react by recognizing that Hashem is with us.

Rabbi Danderovitch of England told this story: A pious man was going on an airplane trip. He requested beforehand to be seated next to a man. However, when he boarded the plane, he saw that the airline had not honored his request. When he politely tried to get the flight attendant to switch his seat, she threatened to throw him off the flight. "And we won't take your luggage off, either," she added angrily.

A non-Jew overheard the argument and told the flight attendant that if she threw the Jewish man off the flight, he would demand to get off too. "And I won't leave without my luggage. You'll have to sift through the whole plane-load to find it."

The flight attendant realized that the situation was only going to snowball. She took a few minutes to find someone willing to switch seats and the problem was settled. The Jewish man later went to the non-Jew to thank him for his support. "You really helped me," he said.

But the non-Jew insisted that he was only protecting himself. He told the man about his friend, a taxi driver in London, who was taking a Jewish man to the airport. The taxi broke down and the driver couldn't fix it. He got another cab to take both him and the passenger to the airport. "I'll make sure you get on your flight even though it's late," the taxi driver promised.

They got to the airport and ran to the gate, but as hard as the taxi driver tried, he could not convince the airline agent to permit the Jewish man to board. The taxi driver apologized to his passenger. He then made his way back to his broken-down cab and turned the key, and it started up like nothing was ever wrong.

A few hours later, he heard the news. Pan Am Flight 103 to New York — the flight his passenger had missed — was blown up by a terrorist as it flew over Scotland.

"From my friend's story," said the non-Jew, "I realized that your G-d protects His people. I felt safe seeing there was a Jew on my flight, and if you were getting off this plane, I was getting off too."

MAKE IT REAL:

When you say, in the blessing over the Torah, "Asher bachar banu mikol ha'amim — Who chose us from all the nations," connect to the feeling of being part of the people Hashem treasures with special love.

21

Easy Payment Plan

Hashem collects His debts with kindness.

When we say, "*Hodu laShem ki tov* — Give thanks to Hashem, for He is good" — we're not setting any conditions for our thanks. We're not saying to thank Him *when* He is good, or *if* He is good. We are saying simply that Hashem, by definition, is good, and therefore, thanking Him is always the right thing to do.

Despite all we've learned about *emunah,* we might still wonder how a human being is supposed to thank Hashem for events that don't feel very good at all. How are we supposed to believe that "Hashem" and "good" are the same thing when life seems to bring us as many reasons to sigh as to smile?

An important understanding we need to have is that we all have an account in Heaven. It registers our sins and our mitzvos, our "debts" and our "deposits." In this world, we have to pay what we owe in full. If you borrow $5 from your friend, he expects $5 in return, and if you can't afford to repay the debt, you are required to pay it as soon as you can. That's simple fairness. You borrow, you owe, and you repay.

Hashem, however, uses a different accounting system. You owe Him $5, but what does He do about it? He gives you $5 so that you have the money to pay Him back. Hashem gives us everything we have and therefore, whatever He takes from us is something He has given us to begin with. If your friend did this for you, you would think of him as the kindest, most generous person you ever knew.

Better still, Hashem allows us to pay huge debts with minor losses and inconveniences. When we experience such a loss, we have to look at it as a favor: maybe we owed Hashem $1,000, but He took only $100 and marked the debt "paid in full."

A mashal: There was a wise man who knew how to understand the language of birds. One day, a man named Yaakov saw the man sitting in a field listening to the birds. "Can you teach me how to do that?" he asked the man.

"It's not a good idea," the wise man said. But Yaakov insisted and finally the wise man agreed. He learned quickly, and finally, he was able to listen to the birds and understand everything they were saying.

His new skill came into good use right away. He heard the birds saying that "Yaakov's warehouse will be destroyed in a fire." Yaakov hired people to empty the warehouse so that when it was burned down the next day, his losses were very slight.

The next day, the birds said the price of silver would drop. Yaakov sold all his silver and prevented a big loss. This bird-language was really helpful!

The day after that, he heard the birds saying that one of Yaakov's stores would be burglarized. Yaakov called the police to guard his store and the burglars never entered. What a fabulous power Yaakov possessed!

Then one night, Yaakov heard the birds saying that "Tomorrow, Yaakov is going to die." Terrified, he ran to the wise man for help.

"I'm sorry, but I warned you that this would not be a good idea. You were supposed to have lost a lot of money from the fire, the drop in silver prices, and the burglary. Now the only way Hashem has for claiming His debt is by taking your life. There's nothing I can do."

Our "bad news" is always an expression of Hashem's love, and always worthy of our gratitude. Knowing we're not perfect, we can be grateful when our "debts" are satisfied with troubles we can endure and overcome.

MAKE IT REAL:

Instead of becoming angry about setbacks in life, say "Thank you, Hashem, that it's this and not something more difficult."

22

Cry on My Shoulder

Even when Hashem gives us troubles, He comforts us.

Two-year-old Yaakov is on the examining table while the doctor prods at his tummy and looks into his ears. After the doctor finishes checking the little boy, he looks at his records and says, "He's due for three shots today."

"Poor little guy," the mother thinks. But she knows that the few moments of tears are worth the protection her child will be receiving against several dangerous diseases.

To prevent Yaakov from moving while the nurse gives him his shots, the mother puts him on her lap and wraps him tightly in her arms. The nurse works swiftly, swabbing his arm and giving the injections: one, two, and three.

Yaakov is screaming in shock and pain. As soon as the nurse is done, his mother holds him a little tighter and speaks calmingly to him. He nestles into her shoulder and continues his crying for a few moments. Then, when she knows he's ready, she distracts him with a toy and all is once again right in his world.

When we think about this very common scenario, we realize that something is strange. The same person who brings the child to the doctor and holds him still so he can receive these painful shots is the one who comforts him in his pain. If we didn't know that the shots were beneficial to the child, we'd think, "What kind of cruel person holds down a helpless child to be stuck with needles?" From the child's point of view, the situation is even more baffling. Here is his mother, the one he trusts and relies on for everything, holding him down so someone can hurt him! Nevertheless, she is the one he turns to for comfort. Somehow, he senses that the pain she's put him through doesn't negate the love she feels for him.

If we can be like this child in our Father's arms, we can have the inner peace and security to get through the painful times that every person experiences. But we have questions that stand in our way: If Hashem loves us, why does He allow people to suffer? Why does He allow sickness and death, mental confusion, financial troubles, and all the other ills of this world? After all, He has the power to simply end all suffering!

We need to know that like the mother in the scenario above, Hashem has compassion on those who suffer pain or loss. "In all their troubles, He was troubled," says the *navi* Yeshayah (63:9). We also need to remind ourselves that for Hashem, it's all one; it's all goodness. The small child cannot understand that the needle-prick protects him from a deadly case of diphtheria. Likewise, a person often cannot know, amid his sadness and suffering, how he is benefiting.

What we *can* know, however, is that our Father is right there, holding us close. He has a shoulder, *kav'yachol,* broad enough for us to lean on as we cry all our tears. When the going gets difficult, our greatest comfort is to feel His embrace and hear His voice telling us, "I love you and I'll help you get through this." When we react to pain by holding on to Hashem more tightly than ever, then no matter what we've lost, we've gained something precious.

MAKE IT REAL:

We build strength for dealing with major challenges by dealing wisely with smaller challenges. When something doesn't go your way and you wonder, "Why, Hashem? Why couldn't You have just given this to me?" rethink your approach. Try instead to hold on to Hashem a little tighter and ask Him to help you get over your hurt.

23

It Would Have Happened Anyway

Cause and effect are only an illusion.

Hashem designed the world so that we would not see His hand busy at work. Instead, He created the system of cause and effect. As we grow up and become educated, we learn: Clouds bring rain and that is why we have water. Seeds sprout and grow, and that's why we have vegetables. Cows give birth to calves, and that's why we have milk and meat. Even more complex are the chains of cause and effect in chemistry, physics, and biology. Someone with a sharp mind and a good education can explain much of what he sees happening in everyday life.

Likewise, history unfolds according to cause and effect. The British placed unfair taxes on the American colonies, and that's why there was a Revolutionary War. Congress voted to end slavery, and that's why America had a Civil War. Islamic militants harbor hatred against the West, and that's why the World Trade Center was destroyed on 9/11.

Life events, too, follow this pattern. A woman has a health issue and that's why she can't have a child. The issue is treated successfully and that's why she is finally able to have a child. A man lacks business skills and that's why he's poor. Another person has wealthy parents and that's why he is rich. A student is easily distracted and that's why he struggles to learn. Another student has a well-focused, intelligent mind and that's why he's a budding *talmid chacham.*

This is how we see life. Whenever something happens, we look for causes and reasons. Sometimes this leads us to take credit for Hashem's kindness: "I thought of this great *shidduch* and now my sister is engaged!" Or, "I studied really hard and I got an A." These statements seem to be very true, but are they?

In fact, they are a reversal of reality. There is no cause for anything other than, "This is what Hashem planned." Something may have happened through our efforts, but it would have happened anyway, through some other means, had we not played our part. As Mordechai says to Esther when she at first resists pleading the Jewish people's cause before King Achashveirosh (*Megillas Esther* 4:14), "If you persist in keeping silent at a time like this, relief and deliverance will come to the Jews from another place..."

This means that the *shidduch* was meant to happen when it did, and that is why her brother thought of the idea when he did. Had he dismissed the idea, someone else would have thought of it. Likewise, the boy who learns well is meant to be a *talmid chacham,* and that is why Hashem gave him a focused and intelligent mind. We also learn from this that when someone is meant to be cured of an illness, Hashem will send the right treatment to the doctor, and when someone is meant to leave the world, no treatment will succeed.

> *As we began writing this sefer, the world was still waiting for a cure to the coronavirus that turned our world upside down starting around Purim 5780 (2020). Baruch Hashem, every day we read about another vaccine or treatment. Hundreds of drug companies are in a race to find the cure. Until it is found, nevertheless, people are being required to wear masks in public places. People are not free to travel from one country to another.*
>
> *People are impatient and frustrated. We read millions of words discussing all the challenges of preventing, treating, and defeating this virus. We learn all about antibodies and immune cells and plasma and hundreds of other details. But there's really only one answer: The crisis will persist and the virus will prowl until Hashem*

takes it away. It may be by means of some treatment now being developed, or it may be by some means no one has yet considered. The end of the story is written, no matter what anyone thinks or does.

For this or anything else we want in life, the only cause is Hashem, and therefore, the most direct path to success is to pray to Him. Sometimes, that's all He is waiting for.

MAKE IT REAL:

When you find yourself thinking about whom to blame or whom to credit for something that has happened, keep in mind that even if the people involved didn't exist, it would have happened anyway.

24

One Way or Another

Hashem always gets us where He wants us to go.

A TRUE STORY

Tzvi drove along the highway. There wasn't much traffic and he was able to speed along smoothly. His speedometer began to creep upward, but he didn't notice — until he saw a police car's flashing lights in his rear-view mirror. His heart sank as he dutifully pulled over.*

"Did you know that you were going 19 miles over the speed limit?" the officer asked him.

"Really, I didn't notice," Tzvi admitted. "I thought I was just riding along at highway speed."

"Well, I know that happens, but I have to give you a ticket," the officer said. "Pay more attention next time."

When Tzvi saw how large the fine was, he became very upset. What a waste of money! He was wondering why this had to happen, when he suddenly realized that the amount of the fine was the same as the amount of ma'aser he owed from his summer job. The next day, he found out that his shul would be sponsoring a fund-raising drive for a chesed organization. He took his ma'aser money and donated it to the cause.

That night, he went onto his computer to pay his fine. It didn't appear in the system. Thinking maybe it was too soon, he waited a week and tried again. It still didn't appear. Neither was it there a month later. Finally, he called the department to pay by phone. "We don't have any record of that ticket," he was told.

Tzvi didn't have to be a prophet to realize that he had gotten a direct message from Hashem: "This amount of money does not belong in your possession. You can give it to *ma'aser* or you can pay it as a fine. One way or another, it will leave your hands." Once he had given the *ma'aser*, the fine was no longer necessary to balance Tzvi's account.

Everything we have is given to us by Hashem so that we can accomplish His purposes. This is true of our money and of our time as well. "Man is born to toil," says *Iyov* (5:7). Work is inevitable. The only question left for us to answer is what work we will do. Chazal teach (*Pirkei Avos* 3:5) that someone who works hard at learning Torah, putting his heart and soul into it since it is his occupation, spares himself some of the efforts he needs to earn a living. Likewise, people who work at helping others can fulfill their quota of work in that way. In both cases, a person is "toiling," but the toil earns the great merit of these mitzvos.

Often, we find it difficult to give away those things that are in our hands, whether it's time, money, our skills and talents, or our possessions. We think that if we don't give the money, we'll have it to buy something we want; if we don't spend the time doing mitzvos or learning, we'll have free time in which to enjoy ourselves. However, those are not options on the menu. The time and money will be spent; the only question is where. When we give of ourselves to accomplish for Hashem, we never lose.

MAKE IT REAL:

If you have trouble motivating yourself to do a chesed, learn Torah, or give tzedakah, remember Tzvi's story and actively choose how your time or money will be used. Remember that you won't gain anything by neglecting to do a mitzvah.

25

Dig Down Deeper

When the answer doesn't come, give Hashem more heart.

In Europe many years ago, there was a group of chassidim who were very poor. Their situation was so bad that they often went hungry. One day, a Rebbe of a different Chassidus came to their town. The group noticed that the Rebbe and his escorts received warm hospitality from many of the families in town. Everyone wanted the honor of hosting the visitors for a meal. This gave them an idea.

They saved whatever little money they could and bought one set of clothing befitting a Rebbe. They chose one man in the group to act the part, and they began traveling from town to town. They would put up posters in each town informing the townspeople of the arrival of the "Rebbe," and as they had hoped, the invitations for lavish meals poured in. They repeated this procedure throughout the area and at last, their days of hunger were over.

Everything went perfectly until one day, they were eating at the home of a wealthy man when his wife came running down the stairs in a state of hysteria. "Rebbe!" she cried. "Our daughter is very ill! You have to save her!"

The "Rebbe" felt a surge of panic. He had no idea what to do, and yet he knew he had to try something. His friends wondered silently whether they might not all be discovered to be imposters.

"Bring the child to a private room," said the "Rebbe." He entered the room, closed the door, and emerged a half-hour later. The girl already looked better. "I think she will be fine," the "Rebbe" said.

When they left the house, the chassidim asked their friend, "How did you do it?"

"I turned to Hashem," he explained, "and I said, 'Hashem, I know that I'm an imposter, a fraud, but I need You. I need You now. Please help me.' I cried from the depths of my heart and prayed with complete sincerity."

When we pray with complete sincerity, recognizing that any and all help that comes into the world comes from Hashem, He is very close to us. As we say in *Ashrei,* "Hashem is close to all who call to Him, to all who call to Him sincerely" (*Tehillim* 145:18). This doesn't mean He is close only to those who are sincere, pure individuals. As we see from the story above, He even answered the prayers of a man who was carrying on a fraud, taking advantage of the innocence and hospitality of Jews who only wanted to honor a visiting Rebbe.

The "Rebbe's" successful attribute was the sincerity of his prayer. He knew without a doubt that if Hashem didn't help him, there was nowhere else to turn. In that spirit, he was able to produce a prayer that effected a miracle.

Sometimes, however, we may question whether this is true. We've all had the experience of praying with all our heart for something important in our lives, and yet with all our prayers and *Tehillim* and *kabbalos,* the answer doesn't come. But this doesn't mean that Hashem isn't close to us. Rather, it means that we can still dig deeper inside us and give Hashem a bit more of our heart. The merit of such a prayer may be what we need to change our situation.

MAKE IT REAL:

If your prayer hasn't been answered, don't give up. Reach out to Hashem from an even deeper place in your heart. Pray as if you're speaking to a person who has the solution in his hand, and if you can just let him know how much you need him to help you, the response is at hand.

26

Your Name in Lights

Greatness is in everyone's reach.

Shimon was a nice, average boy from an average family. He wasn't a great learner. He wasn't a great athlete. He wasn't Mr. Popularity. When he started shidduchim, he expected everything to move along quickly as it did for most of his friends. However, he was having trouble just getting a "yes."

"There's nothing wrong with Shimon," his mother exclaimed to the shadchan after another rejection. "He's the sweetest boy on earth. What's going on?"

"It's not that there's anything wrong," said the shadchan. "It's just that there's nothing outstanding. If a girl is looking for a talmid chacham, that's not him. If she's looking for a guy who's involved in lots of chesed, that's not him. Some girls are looking for a boy who has the drive to succeed in a career, and Shimon's resume doesn't imply that either."

Shimon's mother's heart sank. Her poor son! What would be? But Shimon didn't share his mother's worries. Neither did he share the concerns of his close friends, who lamented, "It's not fair that you're not getting dates! You're the nicest guy. What are girls looking for anyway?"

In Shimon's mind, rejections were a bit disappointing, but in the broader view, they were a blessing. They prevented him from spending time and effort on the wrong girl. He knew very well that the right girl would say "yes." It took about a year for that to happen, but today Shimon is a happy husband and father of five beautiful children, none of whom consider him "average."

In fact, Shimon was not at all average; he was on his way to true spiritual greatness. It just wasn't the kind of greatness a person can describe on a resume. We recognize the greatness of a *talmid chacham,* or a *gadol* who leads his generation and guides them through the ups and downs of life. We also recognize the greatness of people who turn their lives over to serving the Jewish people through acts of *chesed,* and those who start great *chesed* organizations that help thousands of Jews.

However, not everyone has the opportunity to reach greatness in those ways. They may lack certain gifts necessary to make such achievements possible. Even so, there is one path to greatness that is open to every single person, male or female, young or old, of any level of intelligence, money, energy or health. This is the path we travel when we accept Hashem's will in difficult situations. Whenever we don't complain, but instead reach out to Him and say, "I know this is what's best for me, Hashem. Please stay close to me and give me the strength to get through this situation," we've taken a step toward greatness.

This is a reaction we have to work on little by little. The time to build this habit is when the disappointments are small. You get a lower mark on a test than you expected; your Chol HaMoed trip is rained out; your friend cancels plans to spend the day with you; your summer job doesn't come through — if you train yourself to view these types of situations through the perspective of *emunah,* you'll build closeness to Hashem that will enable you to deal with bigger issues the same way.

But why does this add up to greatness? One reason is because accepting Hashem's will with love is considered like bringing an offering to the Beis HaMikdash (Rav Shlomo Kluger, *Kehillas Yaakov, Aseres Yemei Teshuvah* 28). We all pray that Hashem will soon give us the ability to serve Him in this way once more, but until that time, our *emunah* serves the purpose. It's a great *kiddush Hashem* — a statement to ourselves and others that we truly know Hashem is here, running the world with perfection. This is greatness, and it's within our reach.

MAKE IT REAL:

Recognize your progress as you learn to view life more and more through the lens of emunah. Realize that you're not surrendering to a difficult situation but rather, you're winning a major victory.

27

Hashem's Fingerprints

Hashem isn't hidden to those who trust Him.

We know that ever since the Beis HaMikdash was destroyed, Hashem's Presence has been hidden. But sometimes, a situation is so perfectly orchestrated that it's as if Hashem is stepping out from His hiding place and shouting, "Here I am!"

This true story (printed first in *Sha'ah Tova* magazine) told by Rav Chaim Zaid from Yeshivat Nachalat Shelomo in Bnei Brak portrays just such a situation:

One of the Rabbi's students, a 22-year-old boy named Uriel, was diagnosed with a life-threatening brain tumor. After running out of treatment options, the family was told of a doctor in America named Professor Rich, who had a unique surgical technique that was helping patients like Uriel. The only problem was that the surgery would cost $130,000, a sum far out of the family's reach. Also, since Uriel was too sick to travel, the doctor would have to be brought to Israel and given food and housing, adding another $30,000 to the bill. This amount of money was beyond the ability of the local *tzedakah* organizations.

One day, Rav Zaid received a call from Michal Abitbol, who introduced herself as Uriel's sister. She told him that she and her husband had decided to sell their apartment to pay for Uriel's operation. "Please tell the doctor that we're going ahead," she said.

Rav Zaid was concerned. Mrs. Abitbol's husband was a Rabbi who was barely able to support his wife and six children. But Mrs. Abitbol was firm in her decision: "We'll do our part and Hashem will help."

The apartment was sold for $130,000 and the surgery was scheduled. Meanwhile, several of Rabbi Zaid's students donated money toward the remaining $30,000. A few days later, another group of students hired a driver to take them around to collect money. That day, one of the students called Rav Zaid with a question.

"The driver has a suitcase that he wants us to deliver to a certain address," said the student. "Should we do it?"

"Bring the driver here and let me speak to him directly," said Rav Zaid, concerned that something illegal might be going on. However, the driver explained that the bag belonged to a passenger he had picked up earlier that day. It contained strange instruments and seemed to be valuable. He was embarrassed that he hadn't returned it yet, and therefore wanted to send the students to deliver it to the man.

Rav Zaid opened the bag and searched for an identification. He was astounded to discover that the bag belonged to none other than Professor Rich, who had arrived for the surgery. He immediately contacted the surgeon and arranged to meet him in the hotel lobby.

Professor Rich was ecstatic over the find. He thought it was lost for good. "These are the instruments for an operation I came here to perform," he said. "Some of them I designed myself. They're irreplaceable!"

"Something incredible just happened," the Rav told the doctor. "You are here to operate on one of my students, and your bag was found in a car being used by this boy's friends to raise money for the surgery. Surely you see the Divine Providence in this. And you probably also don't know that this operation is only possible because my student's sister sold her home to pay for it. Now she and her husband and six children have no roof over their heads."

Astonished by the intense self-sacrifice of Uriel's family, the doctor decided to waive his fee. The operation went ahead, and it was a success.

Meanwhile, the Abitbol family had to find a home. They decided that this would be a good time to fulfill their dream of living in Yerushalayim, and so their hunt began. However, they soon discovered that $130,000 was far too little. As they were walking the streets, they saw a For Sale sign in an apartment window and decided to check it out. It was just what they needed, but the price, $310,000, was far too high.

"Well, what can you pay?" the owner asked.

"We have $130,000," Rabbi Abitbol said.

"How could you expect an apartment for that?" the man asked.

The Abitbols, sensing the man's frustration, explained why they had sold their home and now found themselves in a tight spot.

"Are you by any chance Mrs. Abitbol?" the man asked.

"Yes!" she answered.

"Unbelievable!" the man responded. "I'm the driver who found the doctor's instruments. I was so impressed when I heard what you had done for your brother. Listen, my mother passed away recently and left me a nice villa in a quiet settlement. That's where I'm moving, and I'm happy to sell you this apartment for whatever you can afford."

> *When we make a sacrifice, counting on Hashem to help us through, we bring berachah into our lives. We show Hashem that we know He's with us and He, in return, gives us even more reason to believe. The more we see Hashem in our lives, the more He comes out of hiding for us.*

MAKE IT REAL:

Whether it's a little extra time or a little extra money, give a little something extra for Hashem with the confidence that it will bring you berachah.

28

Who Are the Heroes?

There are many ways to be brave.

During the peak of the coronavirus pandemic that began around Purim, 5780 (2020), the word "hero" was heard everywhere. Most of the time, it referred to the healthcare workers who were struggling under war-time conditions to care for the thousands of people who fell critically ill. No doubt, the selflessness and hard work of many of those workers, including our own Hatzolah members, made them worthy of that title.

But there were many other heroes as well. They were ordinary people whose family situations suddenly went from average to very, very challenging. They were grandparents who, instead of having a houseful of children and grandchildren for Pesach, had to sit alone at their Seder. They were families whose jobs or businesses closed down, leaving them without money to make Yom Tov or even pay regular bills. Sadly, they were men and women and children, newly widowed or orphaned by the virus, who had to find a way to fulfill "*v'samachta b'chagecha,*" the mitzvah of rejoicing on Yom Tov.

What made these people heroes? Can we compare them to doctors, nurses, and EMTs who ran around 24/7 tending the sick and saving lives, meanwhile exposing themselves to the dangerous virus?

What made them heroes was their willingness to accept their situation and go forward. This doesn't mean they didn't feel the pain. But like a soldier who is shot in the arm but keeps marching forward, they didn't let the pain take them down. Instead, they prayed for strength and tried to find the joy and purpose that was still present in their lives.

Even without coronavirus, many people have family situations that are less than ideal. Someone whose parents are divorced may wish for nothing more than a happy, united family. Someone who feels misunderstood by his parents might wish he got along with them better. Someone with a sibling off the *derech* might wish that he didn't have to deal with his friends' embarrassing comments and questions. Someone whose family has financial troubles might wish he could have all the things that his friends consider "normal."

But none of these situations have to knock us down. The Torah gives us this message through Yaakov Avinu, who earned the title "*bachir she'ba'Avos*" — the choicest of our Forefathers. When we look at his life, however, we may wonder how he even coped. His brother wanted to kill him, his daughter was assaulted by Shechem, and his beloved son was sold into slavery by his own brothers. Dovid HaMelech also had major "family problems" — a father-in-law who tried to kill him, and a son who led a rebellion against him. Difficult family situations are a part of life for many fine, good people. If they grow from them, if they become stronger from them and keep marching forward, they are true heroes.

> *Less than two months after the father had died from coronavirus, his orphaned five-year-old daughter arrived with her mother at a small Bais Yaakov school, where a siddur play was to be held. The mother's eyes gleamed with pride as her little girl took her place on the makeshift stage. Only those who knew how their life had been upended just weeks ago understood the strength on display. The family had suffered and would no doubt continue to suffer their loss, but today was the little girl's special day; there was something to celebrate, and the mother and child let that joy into their hearts.*

Everyone has pain. A hero is someone who realizes that his situation is from Hashem and his pain will help him grow.

Instead of becoming despondent and hiding from the world, or becoming angry and full of resentment, a hero marches on. We saw during the coronavirus that a hero can be a 70-year-old Bubbi, a 5-year-old girl, or a 40-year-old store owner. A hero can be you.

MAKE IT REAL:

When things don't go your way, ask yourself, would you rather be a victim of circumstance or a hero?

29

"What's in It for Me?"

The one who trusts in Hashem is surrounded by kindness.

One of the most confusing parts of life is when our good ideas and good intentions don't bring us the good results we hoped for. We would think that if we're doing what Hashem wants of us, He should make our efforts successful. At the very least, we shouldn't end up in a worse position because of it. Yet sometimes, it seems that Hashem Himself is stopping us from doing a mitzvah or improving ourselves.

For example, you decide as you begin a new school year that this year, you're going to stay on top of your homework. No more waiting until the last minute. No more rush jobs. No more begging for an extension. You're going to be a conscientious student. Your teachers will be pleased with you, your grades will soar, your parents will be delighted, and your friends will notice how you really got yourself together.

Then what happens? In the second week of school, you come down with the flu. You miss seven days of classes. You fall far behind; the situation is worse than ever! Doesn't Hashem want you to learn well? Doesn't He want you to become more responsible? Why does it seem as if He threw you off track?

At a moment like this, our *emunah* is being tested. And what is the correct answer to this test? "For the one who trusts in Hashem kindness surrounds him," says Dovid HaMelech

(*Tehillim* 32:10). This is the moment to strengthen our trust in Hashem and tell ourselves that although the situation didn't work out as we had planned, Hashem is leading us where we need to go. We have to make ourselves like a baby snug in his stroller, relaxed and totally reliant on the One Who is pushing us along. Like the baby, we don't have the wisdom to judge whether the route we're on is the best one. The baby doesn't even know where his mother is taking him!

The *pasuk* above is telling us that when we relax and put our faith in Hashem's guidance, even if He seems to be derailing our good intentions, this brings His blessings and kindness. Our job is not to decide how things should happen, but rather, to go forward with our best intentions and trust that the result is exactly as Hashem has decided it should be, all for our benefit. As long as our intentions are good and we are acting with the Torah and wiser people as our guide, we've done our part.

Rabbi Fischel Schachter tells a story of Rabbi Eliyahu Lopian that perfectly illustrates this point:

> *Rabbi Lopian's yeshivah in Kelm was in desperate need of funds. Therefore, he personally traveled soliciting support. At last he managed to raise the needed amount, but the situation at the yeshivah was so desperate that they could not wait for his arrival. He instructed those responsible for paying the yeshivah's debts to take out a loan for the amount needed, since he had the money in hand and could pay back the loan immediately.*
>
> *Now Rabbi Lopian just needed to board a train and go back to Kelm. He asked a man for directions to the station and the man offered to escort him the entire way. The man led him into a dark alleyway. "Are you sure this is the right way?" the Rabbi asked. The man reassured him that it was. Moments later, however, the man pulled out a gun and seized all the money Rabbi Lopian was carrying. Now the yeshivah was in extreme straits and there was nothing with which to repay their debt.*
>
> *Rabbi Lopian didn't question Hashem. He simply devised a "Plan B," which was to get back on the road and raise the money again. Inexplicably, he decided to*

go to England. The Jews there were deeply inspired by this Lithuanian Rabbi and his extraordinary wisdom. Not only did they respond warmly to his fundraising efforts, but also, they asked him to remain as a Rabbi in London. He accepted, moved his family to London, and became Rosh Yeshivah of Yeshivas Etz Chaim.

Thus, Rabbi Lopian and his family became the only survivors of the destruction that the Nazis brought to his town after he left. He lived into his 90s and brought 13 children into the world, many of them leading Torah figures in their own right.

Rabbi Schachter points out that Rabbi Lopian was saved by his *emunah*. He trusted in Hashem when it seemed that Hashem was rejecting his noble efforts and as a result, as Dovid HaMelech promised, he was "surrounded by kindness."

MAKE IT REAL:

Practice the habit of "suspending judgment" when Hashem sends you off in a direction you don't understand. Rather than complaining or feeling that Hashem is against you, tell yourself to relax and see where He is taking you.

30

"Count Me In!"

Hashem cares that we care.

You're walking down the street on a snowy day when you spot an elderly man standing outside his stuck car. Two of your classmates are pushing the car while another sits at the wheel, pressing the gas pedal. The car wheels have dug themselves into an icy rut and your friends are trying to push it out. You run over to join them in their good deed. "Let me get in there," you say to the two who are pushing the back bumper. "You need more manpower."

When we see others trying to help someone, our *yetzer tov* wants to join in. Where we might have otherwise walked by the stuck car thinking, "Poor guy. I hope he gets out of this," instead we are activated to join in the rescue mission. And in this way, we are acting as Hashem does.

During the Jewish people's enslavement in Egypt, Hashem said (*Shemos* 6:5), "I also have heard the groans of *Bnei Yisrael*." The *sefer Ki Ata Imadi* brings us a question from earlier commentators: Why did Hashem say "also"? Who else heard the groans?

The answer is that the Jewish people heard each other's groans of pain and felt compassion for each other, even though they were all suffering. When they saw each other's pain, they sincerely wished that it would cease; they therefore prayed to Hashem for the other person. They each felt that they would be happy to see the other person's suffering relieved, even if they themselves still suffered. Hashem, seeing the care of one Jew for the other, knew that this was the right time and circumstance for Him to push their redemption forward.

We often hear Chazal's (*Bava Kamma* 92a) statement that when we pray for another person who has the same need we have, we will be answered first. This may be why: Hashem sees our concern for someone else who is suffering what we are suffering, and because of the great merit of that brotherly love, He joins the rescue.

But this merit is only as great as the sincerity in the person's heart. If he is praying for the other person specifically because that will bring him his own *yeshuah,* then the merit is far less. This is also the case if the other person's *yeshuah* upsets him and gives him a pang of envy. For someone to pray sincerely, he has to really feel, "I know what it's like to suffer with his problem. I would be so happy to see him freed from it."

This is not an easy level to reach. For example, imagine a student who finds studying difficult. She spends hours at it and never gets better than a C. Her best friend has the same situation, and the two of them often share their frustrations. Then one day, the friend begins studying with a new tutor, who helps her to break through her barriers. Suddenly her grades are climbing and the other students in the class are looking at her with new respect. Can the poor student who is still struggling really feel happy for her friend's success?

The best response she could have would be, "*Baruch Hashem,* I'm so glad she doesn't have to have so much frustration from schoolwork anymore." It takes a lot of training and focus on building *ahavas Yisrael* to make this our default reaction. But if we do, we invite Hashem to say, "Your attitude is so beautiful. I want to be part of it."

Our best approach to difficulties in life is to use our pain and frustration to feel for others. By giving us the same challenge, Hashem is showing us how they feel, and we can turn that lesson into sincere prayers for them. In this way, we grow tremendously from our difficulties. Their purpose is thus fulfilled, and Hashem can whisk them away.

MAKE IT REAL:

Think of an issue in your life. Do you know someone else who is dealing with the same issue, maybe even more intensely than you are? Find it in your heart to feel for that person and imagine his happiness at having the issue resolved. Then pray for him.

31

The BIG Emunah Question

Each piece of the puzzle is part of a breathtaking picture

Rivka, 19, has loads of energy and she tries to use it productively. She works full-time and takes courses at night. In whatever spare time she has, she volunteers at a school for special-needs children.

One summer Friday afternoon, the mother of Dina, one of the special-needs children, calls Rivka and asks her a favor. "My son fell and needs stitches. I have to take him to the emergency room, and I need someone to watch Dina. You're the only one she feels comfortable with, so it would be an amazing help if you could come over and stay with her while I'm at the hospital. I hope it won't take too long and anyway, Shabbos isn't for another five hours."

Kind-hearted Rivka agrees immediately. While she does have a lot of schoolwork she was hoping to catch up on that afternoon, it will just have to wait. Soon she's pushing Dina on a backyard swing while Dina's mother and brother head to the emergency room. An hour later, Dina's mother calls to say that the emergency room is packed. "I'm so sorry," she says. "We'll get home in time iy"H, but it's going to be close."

Finally, the mother and son return. It's 15 minutes before candle-lighting when Dina heads home. She has just turned onto the main road when she hears the thump-thump-thump of a flat tire. Now what? She calls her father in a panic. He advises her to pull the car over into a safe spot where it can stay for Shabbos. He speeds to her rescue and brings her home.

If Dina's first thought is a frustrated complaint of, "Is this what I get for doing a mitzvah?" she won't be alone. Many people feel betrayed by Hashem when they run into a setback after doing a mitzvah. We expect our good deeds to be rewarded with good, not with added difficulties. Because our belief in reward and punishment and our trust in Hashem's justice is such a major part of our *emunah,* these situations present us with a big challenge.

One of the most commonly asked questions in *hashkafah* is, "Why do bad things happen to good people?" The simple answer is that, as we know, our mitzvos are not really rewarded in this world (*Sefer BaYam Derech*). The reward is so far beyond the limits of our physical world that it cannot be given here. The "bad things" are often a further test, through which our reward in the Next World will be even greater.

Let's imagine how Avraham Avinu must have felt when he returned from *Akeidas Yitzchak* — one of the greatest examples ever of doing Hashem's will without question — and discovers that Sarah has died. Worse yet, she died when she was told that her husband had gone to offer their son as a sacrifice. Who could blame Avraham if he thought, "This doesn't make sense! I just undertook the biggest test of my life and Hashem rewards me by taking away my wife?" Rabbeinu Yonah says that in fact, Sarah's death was a continuation of the test, which Avraham passed. He never doubted Hashem.

When we look at one piece of a 1,000-piece puzzle, we can't make sense of it; only when we see it as part of the whole picture do we understand that it plays a crucial role. When Mashiach comes, soon *iy"H,* we will be able to see the whole picture, but until then, we can build our *emunah* by trusting that each piece of the puzzle is part of a breathtaking picture, perfectly designed by Hashem.

MAKE IT REAL:

Instead of feeling that you've lost by doing a mitzvah, imagine the reward being deposited in a secret savings account that will grow beyond your wildest dreams throughout your whole life.

32

More Than You Could Ask For

Always ask, "Who sent this present?"

When we stop to think about what our parents do for us, we're amazed. Imagine waking up every night, maybe even several times a night, in the dark and the cold, getting out of your warm bed, taking a crying infant out of his crib, spending a half-hour feeding him and then putting him back to sleep. Imagine doing that not just one night, but every night for months.

Imagine getting up every day before the sun comes up, going to shul, then going to an office and working hard the entire day, from morning to night. You earn a nice amount of money for your efforts, but you barely keep any of it for yourself. Instead, you use it to pay for a house big enough for your family to live in, food to feed them all, tuition for their yeshivos and camps, clothing for them all and so forth. If you were to keep all the money you made for yourself, you'd have millions in the bank. But you're happy to spend it all on others.

Amazingly, we almost never realize what our parents do for us. We don't tend to see dinner on the table and think, "Wow, my mother really loves me." We don't see the lights and air conditioning operating in our home and think, "Wow, Daddy works so hard to keep our house running. He really loves us." What we *do* notice, however, are the gifts and special treats our parents give us: the presents, trips, and special privileges. The "extras" people give us shine a bright light on their love and care. We know they're thinking of us and aiming to make us happy.

For this reason, one powerful way to strengthen our sense of Hashem's love is to notice all the "extras" He sends into our life. We can and should thank Him for the air we breathe and the functioning of our bodies and the millions of other acts of kindness He pumps into our life every minute of the day, but as in the case of a child and his parents, these gifts become part of "the way it is" and are easy to take for granted. We would be cheating ourselves out of a great source of happiness, however, if we failed to notice the extras.

For instance, when something turns out better than we had expected, or someone helps us out in some way, or we achieve a goal that seemed out of reach — or any time we receive more than we actually need — we should stop and notice. It's Hashem sending us a gift with a note attached that says, "Here is a special gift for my child." If a gift came to the door, the first thing we would want to know is, "Who sent this?" We would want to know who thought of us and went out of his way to make us happy. The gift itself might make us happy for a while, but the idea that someone took the time and care to send it to us gives us happiness that lasts far longer.

A True Story

Dena, a divorced woman who raised six children on her own, lost her 25-year-old son to cancer. In the months that she was caring for him, she wasn't able to keep her regular work hours, which meant less money and brand-new piles of debt. Now her daughter Debbie was getting married. She wanted Debbie to have all the new clothing a kallah should have, but due to money concerns, she knew that their choices would be confined to sales and gemachs. But wouldn't it be wonderful, Dena thought, if we could just walk into a nice dress store and Debbie could pick out what she wanted? Dena had always counted on Hashem's help, and she still did. She prayed that somehow, she would be able to marry her daughter off without strain.

Not long after that, Debbie met Rena, a friend of her boss. Rena was helping another friend promote a line *of elegant clothing. When Rena heard that Debbie was engaged, she said, "I can't believe this! My friend gave me a $1,000 gift certificate for her clothing line and told me to give it to a kallah. It's yours!"*

That evening, Debbie was in shopping bliss, choosing from beautiful, stylish dresses for her Sheva Berachos wardrobe. When another customer — a wealthy member of the community — heard that someone had provided a $1,000 gift certificate, she wanted to add another $1,000. Debbie had what she needed, so she called her mother to come shop. The mother and daughter were regally outfitted for their simchah. Dena, who had suffered so much hardship, found special joy in the feeling that Hashem was pampering her with elegant clothing that were not an absolute necessity.

"It feels like Hashem, as it were, is giving us a hug, saying, 'Don't worry. I am taking care of everything,'" Dena said.

MAKE IT REAL:

Make a list of 10 "extras" Hashem has provided for you. Imagine that each is a thoughtful gift sent to your doorstep by Someone Who loves you.

33

Don't Ignore the Message

When trouble strikes, look inside.

Have you ever walked through a maze? The goal is to get out on the other side, but you can't see your destination. The only way to find the exit is to follow the path until you reach a dead end, and then turn onto the next available path. You keep bumping into dead ends as you make your way through the maze. But you don't think to yourself, "These annoying dead ends are getting in my way," and just stop there. Instead, you think, "I took a wrong turn. I have to try this other path." The barriers are a message that says, "You're heading in the wrong direction."

The same is true when we "bump into barriers" in our life. We want something, we pursue it with all our heart, and then Hashem throws an obstacle in our way. For example, a young lady wants to get married. She is fortunate to receive a "yes" from many prospects, but one after the other, they just don't work out. She feels that she's banging into one wall after another, when all she wants is to get to the other side — a marriage and family.

But as each day passes, she grows. She becomes less self-centered. Her priorities become clearer. She prays with more sincerity and Hashem becomes a bigger part of her life. After two years of dating, she meets her *bashert*. All the new qualities she has developed as she bumped into walls and tried new paths have made her into a girl suited to this idealistic young man who is eager to spend years learning Torah, and enabled her to build a family with the ideal *hashkafos*. Now the girl realizes that every time Hashem blocked her path, He was telling her, "You've got work to do before you're ready for your real *bashert*!"

When Hashem sends us inconveniences and disappointments, His purpose is often to cause us to reconsider the path we're on. That's why the Gemara tells us that when a person is having troubles in life, he should think about his actions and habits and look for ways to improve. But we might think, "What if I make a commitment to improve something and my trouble stays the same?"

There are no guarantees, and no one has the power of a *navi* to say, "Here's what's wrong and here's what you need to do." But there is no doubt that improving ourselves in the way we serve Hashem or deal with other people will always help us in some area. And sometimes, Hashem does us the amazing kindness of telling us exactly what needs to be improved.

A True Story

A young woman got married, but after three years, still didn't have children. At that time in her life, she lit Shabbos candles but did not keep Shabbos according to halachah. Someone advised her to try to observe the laws of the Torah more carefully as a merit for having a child. She began to pray every day, make berachos before eating, and turn off her phone on Shabbos. Eventually, she had a baby boy. After that, the family grew.

One Friday evening, she tried to light her Shabbos candles but only one of the two would light. She kept trying, but the second wick wouldn't catch fire. The same thing happened for several weeks and it was beginning to frighten her. What could it mean? She called her Rabbi, and he suggested that it might be a sign for her to go a little further and stop watching television on Shabbos. The woman thought her husband and children would object, so she looked for some other merit that might fix the situation.

But nothing helped. Each week, one candle would

light up and the other would keep going out. Finally, she told her family about the Rabbi's suggestion and they agreed to shut the television for Shabbos. That Friday night, not only did both candles remain lit, but the flames burned brighter and taller than ever before.

To hear Hashem's message in our troubles, we have to keep our minds open. Our heart usually knows what needs to be done, but we may block out its voice with thoughts of, "How do I know that will help? Maybe it's something else." Instead, we can think, "Hashem is bothering to reach into my life and tell me something. What is the message?"

MAKE IT REAL:

Is there a challenge that keeps coming up in your life? Think about a few ways you could learn and grow from it and make a commitment to take one small step in that direction.

34

How About a "Thank You"?

There's a blessing behind every difficulty.

The Rothenbergs take their eight children on a big Chol HaMoed trip to an amusement park. The children have a full day of fun flying around on all kinds of twisty, stomach-dropping roller coasters. The younger children enjoy pony rides and a merry-go-round.

At the end of the day, the children want to "cash in" prize tickets they won at some of the carnival games. Seven-year-old Eliyahu is disappointed to discover that he is 10 tickets short of a walkie-talkie he wants. He tries to talk his five-year-old sister into handing over 10 of her tickets with the promise that the walkie-talkie will belong to both of them. She, however, has her eye on a princess crown. The negotiations soon turn into a fight, which soon turns into tears.

The commotion irritates the older children, who also begin complaining. The parents, who had set out for the day filled with high hopes for a happy family outing, wonder, "What's the point? We spent a gazillion dollars and hours running around the park just to give the kids a good time, and now they're all going home unhappy. We might just as well have stayed home."

Nobody wants to give to someone who is ungrateful. If our attempts at kindness are always answered with a complaint about the part that's not quite perfect, we will give up trying to please that person. There's no point.

If we don't train our eyes to see what there is to be grateful for in life, we may end up like those crying, bickering children, ignoring the gifts we've been given and screaming about the one thing that's missing. This is the wrong way to ask Hashem to give us more. Just like the parents in our scenario, He will realize that no matter what He gives us, it won't be satisfactory. Rather than putting a stumbling block in front of us, providing opportunity after opportunity to ignore His goodness and take Him for granted, He'll stop giving.

We need to be grateful not only for what goes right, but even for what goes wrong. Every challenge contains a *chesed* in it. For example, if a person has the flu, he can thank Hashem for giving him an illness that heals, rather than one that can't be cured. If someone's younger sibling is throwing a tantrum, he can thank Hashem that he's part of a family; imagine being all alone! If someone has trouble with learning, he can thank Hashem that he has the intelligence to improve, or teachers and tutors who can help him, or even the freedom to learn Torah, which many generations before us did not have.

In *Tehillim* (85:8), Dovid HaMelech says, "Show us Your kindness, Hashem, and grant us Your salvation." Commentators teach that this means that by seeing Hashem's kindness, we affect our salvation. This is as Yaakov Avinu taught us when he was about to face Esav (*Bereishis* 32:11) and said, "[Hashem,] I am diminished by all the kindnesses...that [You have done for Your servant]." Only after he acknowledged Hashem's kindnesses did he ask Hashem to protect him from Esav. If we look at Yaakov's life, however, we see that he had already gone through many struggles; he had to flee from Esav and deal with all of Lavan's tricks and deception. But he didn't say, "Now what, Hashem? How much more do I have to go through?" He thanked Hashem for all the good in his life, recognizing that Hashem owed him nothing at all. With gratitude in his heart, he asked for Hashem's continued help, and it was granted.

Thanking Hashem in the midst of our difficulties can turn

everything around for us. We are happier people when we focus on the goodness we enjoy in life. This gives us the right approach to our *tefillos,* and very often, as Dovid HaMelech taught, it brings us the answer to our trouble.

MAKE IT REAL:

The next time you feel like reacting with frustration to a problem, think of the good the problem represents. For instance, you can't spill your coffee if you couldn't afford coffee.

35

A Tap on the Shoulder

Hashem's acts of kindness are tailor-made.

A TRUE STORY

A mother named Hannah worked at a computer job to earn money for her children's yeshivah tuition. Because she was a very devoted mother, she left her house at 4:45 in the morning so that she could get her work done and be home when her children returned from school. The only way for her to leave so early was to have a live-in babysitter who would be available as soon as the children woke up.

The plan worked well for about six months. Then, Hannah started noticing that the babysitter was losing patience with her little boy, who was too young to complain to his mother. Hannah knew that if the babysitter was being impatient right in front of her, she was probably worse when Hannah was at work. The mother immediately fired the babysitter and decided to ask her boss if she could do her computer work from home.

The boss said, "absolutely not." In fact, he said, no one would hire her to work from home. Now Hannah was stuck. She worked so that her children could have a yeshivah education, but she would never again consider leaving her children alone with a stranger. Then she realized that this problem wasn't hers to solve. She turned to Hashem and spoke to Him about her worries.

"Please send me a job I can do from home so that I can pay for my children's yeshivah and also keep them safe!" she pleaded, tears filling her eyes.

One week later, someone called to offer her a job. It was far from her home, but that didn't matter; the organization would allow her to work from home. Just in case Hannah didn't realize that Hashem was listening to her prayers and arranging a solution for her, He provided a hint — a tap on the shoulder that said, "Here I am." And what was that tap? It was the name of the organization that hired Hannah: Save the Children.

Hashem wants us to know that we're never facing a situation alone. For example, when we're stepping through the door of yeshivah or high school for the first time, nervous about all the new rules, new people, longer days, and more difficult work, we can feel confident that Someone great and powerful is walking right by our side. And if we pay attention, we'll see that throughout those first few days, He is tapping us on the shoulder, helping us make new friends and adjust to our new environment in dozens of small ways. A rebbi called on you to answer a question on the topic you just studied with your father last night? That's a tap on the shoulder. A girl in the seat next to you turns out to be an old friend from camp? That's a tap on the shoulder. Your favorite lunch was served at school today? That's a tap on the shoulder too.

The more we notice that Hashem is right there with us, the more we'll call on Him to help us and thank Him when He does. Because calling on Him and thanking Him are the keys to having our prayers answered; we are automatically helping to improve our situation by remembering that He's there with us. This doesn't mean that all our problems are instantly solved, but it does mean that we never have to feel that we're facing a problem alone. We always have support, love, and concern, and it comes from the One Who can actually make our situation better. When we look for those taps on the shoulder, we truly live with Hashem.

MAKE IT REAL:

Today, be on the lookout for "taps on the shoulder" — times Hashem sends you a kindness that seems specially meant to tell you He's there.

36

Let's Be Friends

Hashem can make us love and be loved.

A scenario: *In ninth grade, Dovi and Dani were such close friends that their classmates referred to them as D&D. They shared a lot of jokes and liked the same music and books. In the spring, both boys applied to an overnight camp in the mountains. "We'll only go if we both get in," Dovi told Dani, who agreed to the plan. However, when Dani got in and Dovi did not, that plan was forgotten.*

"But you said..." Dovi began to argue.

"Yeah, but my parents want me to go," said Dani. "Besides, who says we have to go everywhere together? Maybe it will be good to make some other friends."

Dovi was deeply hurt. Little by little, D&D came apart. Dani wondered why Dovi couldn't understand how foolish he would be to give up his place in this fantastic camp that everyone wanted to attend. Why was he so self-centered? Dovi wondered how Dani could just back out of his agreement like that and ruin his summer in the process.

Despite the justifications each boy made for his coldness to the other boy, they both felt miserable about the loss of their friendship. They weren't actually in a feud; they still spoke to each other and spent time together, but it was far from what it used to be.

Reading this scenario, we might think that the friendship is over. These two boys will never be close again. However, if that is what we think, then we are leaving Hashem out of the picture. The way people feel about others is in His hands. As Shlomo HaMelech (*Mishlei* 16:7) tells us, "When a person finds favor in Hashem's eyes, even his enemies will make peace with him." If we ever want to make peace with someone but that person is not interested, we can ask Hashem to soften that person's heart. Likewise, if we start finding someone in our life irritating, we can ask Him to soften our heart and restore our positive feelings.

Can Hashem really reach inside a person's heart and determine how he feels? We know from the Torah that Hashem influenced the feelings of the Egyptians. After Yosef had served the country so well and saved the people from famine, we might think that the Jewish people would be honored residents of Egypt. Instead, "Hashem turned their hearts to hate His nation" (*Tehillim* 105:25). In addition, we know that He "hardened the heart" of Pharaoh many times during the Ten Plagues. Then, after suffering the plagues brought by Moshe and Aharon, the Egyptians willingly turned over their wealth to their former slaves. Why? The Torah explains that "Hashem gave the [Jewish] people favor in the eyes of the Egyptians" (*Shemos* 12:36).

Likewise, when Esav was leading a troop of 400 men to attack Yaakov, Hashem turned Esav's hatred into love. Esav hugged his brother and offered to travel with him. Rashi (*Bereishis* 33:4) explains that "Esav's mercy was aroused at that moment." Yaakov had prayed for help in dealing with Esav, and Hashem answered him by stirring Esav's brotherly feelings. He had hated Yaakov before their meeting and hated him again forever after, but at that moment, he felt no desire to harm him.

Often, we come across difficult people in our lives. There might be a teacher who seems strict and demanding, a fellow student who is unfriendly toward us — even a family member with whom we seem to have trouble getting along. Of course, there are many practical ways to try to improve difficult relationships, but we should never forget that Hashem can open up another person's eyes to our positive qualities and influence them to value us. If we live in a way that pleases Hashem and ask Him to help us, He will influence others to be pleased with us. Peace with others is something well worth our *tefillos*.

MAKE IT REAL:

Is there a relationship in your life that could use improvement? Daven to Hashem once a day to help you and that person see each other in a positive light.

37

You Won't Lose by Giving

Let Hashem do the math.

Everyone who has ever learned simple arithmetic knows that if you have 100 pennies and you give five to your friend, you now have 95 pennies. If you want to buy something that costs a dollar, you probably won't be willing to give those five pennies away.

That's how it works in the physical world. Everything is limited, and therefore, when we give something, we have less of it. This is even the case with things we can't actually hold and touch, like time. When we're in a hurry, we feel that we can't "afford" to take a few minutes to do someone a favor.

All of this seems as simple and obvious as the sun in the sky. However, when we limit our *chesed* because we're afraid that giving to someone else will leave us lacking what we need, we are forgetting the basic lesson of *emunah*. That is that Hashem gives us everything we need, and Hashem has no limits. When we do what He wants of us, He makes sure that we won't lack anything. Either He will return to us what we've given away, or He will show us that our good deed has taken us in a different but better direction than we had planned.

You may have seen this yourself. Your friend asks you for a favor just as you're about to do something else. You think, "I don't have time," but instead, you push yourself to do the right thing and say, "Sure I'll help you out." Most of the time when this happens, you discover that you still have plenty of time to do what you had originally planned. Sometimes you find that the delay that was caused by you stopping to help your friend ended up helping you in some unexpected way. For instance, you drive your friend to pick up his shirts at the dry cleaner and while you're there, you suddenly remember that your father had asked you to pick up his shirts as well.

Of course, we have to be responsible and use our time wisely. We need to ensure that we have the time and the money available to fulfill our responsibilities. However, there's often at least a little "wiggle room" for us to help others when it's not exactly convenient or comfortable to do so. That's when we need to tell ourselves, "I'll do the job Hashem just put in front of me and He'll make sure it all works out."

A True Story

One Erev Pesach, Shulamit was busy getting her house ready for a giant Seder. She and her husband often invited people who were becoming religious, and on this Seder night, two Jewish families from Russia were expected. She had purchased haggadahs with Russian translations for the occasion. But as she worked on her preparations, her heart was heavy. Her best friend Naava's mother had passed away the day before and today was the funeral. Shulamit did as much as she could to set up for the Seder and then she and her husband flew out of the house to the funeral home.*

It was supposed to be a brief levayah, because there are no hespedim (speeches honoring the person who has died) on Erev Yom Tov. However, Naava's brother couldn't hold back his words. The minutes ticked by and then there were two more relatives who had "a few words to say." Finally, it was time to go to the cemetery for burial. Shulamit noticed that no one was accompanying Naava and her husband to the cemetery. After all, everyone had to rush home to get ready for the Seder.

"We should go with her," said Shulamit's husband.

"I want to," Shulamit said, "but we'll be getting home so late. The cemetery is at least an hour away."

Even so, they decided that they couldn't let Naava go through this sad moment without any friends at her side.

They got on the highway and it was jammed.

"Don't worry," said her husband. "Hashem will shorten the road for us on the way home."

"You're dreaming," said Shulamit.

They went to the cemetery and Shulamit stood by Naava's side and comforted her as her mother was laid to rest. Then she and her husband headed home. Amazingly, the highway that had been jammed with cars an hour earlier was free and clear. They were home in plenty of time to finish their preparations and even grab a nap before candle-lighting.

MAKE IT REAL:

The next time you feel you need to say "no" to a chesed because it's a little too much for you, push yourself to say "yes" and then take note: Did it work out after all?

38

It's Worth the Wait

Trust and patience bring peace and happiness.

The idea of *emunah* rests on our belief that Hashem loves us, can do anything, and only wants to do good. But when something in our life is not as we want it to be, these beliefs can become shaky. Where is the good? Who says it's coming?

The skill we need to develop in order to have true, strong *emunah* is patience. Dovid HaMelech tells us throughout *Tehillim* that patiently waiting for Hashem to show us the way, knowing that He certainly will, is the only way to live in peace.

"*Nafshi Ladonai mishomrim laboker* — My soul [yearns] for Hashem more than a watchman [yearns] for morning" (*Tehillim* 130:6). The night watchman keeps his eyes peeled for the first hint of dawn, the first narrow line of light that peeks over the horizon. As he watches and waits, he never thinks, "What if the sun doesn't rise today?" He doesn't say, "I'm sick of waiting and waiting for nothing." He knows that the sun will rise, and it will be at exactly the right time, and then his work will be finished.

That's the patient confidence we need when we're waiting for Hashem to show us the light that will help us through our difficult times. We have to know that it's coming, even if it hasn't peeked over the horizon yet. And we have to know that it will not come one second before Hashem is ready to show it to us.

A TRUE STORY

Many years ago, Mr. Goldstein was traveling from London to Eretz Yisrael for Yom Kippur. The passenger next to him was a non-religious Jew named Mr. Schechter. Striking up a conversation with Mr. Schechter, Mr. Goldstein found out that he was a Holocaust survivor who was angry at Hashem. The man had asked one thing of Hashem, which was that his young son would survive the war. But the Nazis took away his son and he never saw him again. To Mr. Schechter, this showed that Hashem did not care about him, and therefore, he wanted nothing more to do with Torah or mitzvos.

Just how far Mr. Schechter took his feud with Hashem became obvious on Yom Kippur. Mr. Goldstein had been in shul davening. The chazzan was exceptional and the tefillos had been very inspiring. When the time came to say Yizkor, the prayer for deceased parents, Mr. Goldstein left the shul along with all the others whose parents were still living. He spotted Mr. Schechter sitting on a bench near the shul, munching on a sandwich.

Shocked as Mr. Goldstein was, he still went to greet him. Then he suggested that even if he didn't want to pray, perhaps he could just go inside the shul and say Yizkor for his son. After a little more convincing, Mr. Schechter agreed to do so for his son's sake.

He approached the chazzan to give him his son's name — Yaakov.

"And your name?" the chazzan asked.

"Moshe. My son was Yaakov ben Moshe," Mr. Schechter said.

The chazzan stopped for a moment and then asked, "What is your last name?"

Mr. Schechter couldn't imagine why the chazzan needed to know this, but he told him, "It's Schechter."

The chazzan's eyes filled with tears as he looked at the sad, broken man standing in front of him.

"Dad? Is it you? Where were you? I've been looking for you for 37 years!" the chazzan cried.

The two men hugged and cried in each other's arms,

with the rest of the shul crying right along. Mr. Schechter eventually returned to Torah and mitzvos.

Not every situation is solved with a miracle like the one in this story. But think of what Mr. Schechter's life would have been like if, instead of giving up on Hashem, he had trusted Him that He was leading him on a good path in life. Instead of 37 years of bitterness, he would have had 37 years of sweetness, connecting to Hashem and other people with trust and love. Waiting for Hashem's light to peek out and shine into our lives is a sure bet, always worth the wait.

MAKE IT REAL:

Imagine that the help you want from Hashem is like a delicious soup cooking on the stove. It's already in the making, but won't be ready for you until it's perfect.

39

I'll Lend You the Money You Owe Me

Why give it only to take it back?

You go out for a slice of pizza with your friend. When you get to the cashier, you dig into your pocket and realize that you didn't take any money with you. Your friend sees what's happening and says, "Don't worry. I'll pay and you can pay me back."

The next day, you see your friend coming toward you and you're embarrassed. You forgot to bring him the money you owe. He comes over to you, digs into his pocket and says, "Here, take this $2.50."

"But I owe *you* $2.50," you tell him, feeling rather confused.

"I know!" he says. "That's why I'm giving you the money. Now you have the $2.50 you need to pay me back."

If this were a business transaction, it wouldn't make sense. The friend has laid out $5 in order to get back $2.50. But this is how Hashem, in His kindness, sometimes does business with us. We see this in action when something good comes our way and then He takes it back. For instance, a boy in *shidduchim* goes out with a girl several times and everything seems perfect. He thinks, "Finally, I found my *bashert*!" Then the *shadchan* tells him that the girl does not want to go forward. The boy is not only disappointed, but angry. "Why did Hashem put this in my hands only to snatch it back? It would have been so much easier if she saw right away that I wasn't for her."

When we experience this type of situation, we should understand that we needed some type of *kapparah* and our disappointment serves that purpose. Hashem knows what we can withstand. If He sees that we don't have the resources to "pay what we owe," then He puts those resources in our hands. Then He takes them back. This, like everything else Hashem does, is for our benefit. A person who has this kind of trust in Hashem gains even when he seems to have been left empty-handed, as this true story from Rabbi Elimelech Biderman illustrates:

> *The father of a large family was struggling with debts and had many children to marry off. Occasionally, he took his chances on a lottery ticket. One day, he received a call telling him that he had won. He would receive millions of shekels! That Shabbos, the family was floating on air. Their table was filled with songs and words of praise to Hashem. But on Sunday, the father received another call from the lottery office telling him that they had made a mistake. Someone else had won.*
>
> *Instead of falling into depression, the father taught his children a lesson in emunah. "Chazal (Sefer HaMaasiyos L'Rabbeinu Nissim Gaon, citing Batei Midrash 8:6) say that when Hashem issues a decree of illness or death on a person, He sometimes takes money or possessions instead of the person's life. But what if the person doesn't have money? Then He makes it appear as if the person has money and then takes that away. The person earns his kapparah without losing anything."*

The father realized that what seemed like cruelty — getting the family's hopes up only to have them crash down again — was in fact a great kindness. We may not be able to see the details of Hashem's accounting system — for instance, what sin needs atonement and what decree might have been coming our way — but with simple trust in Hashem, we can be sure that we always come out ahead.

MAKE IT REAL:

The next time you experience a disappointment, remind yourself that Hashem is allowing you to "pay Him back with His own money."

40

Reverse the Charge

A little emunah builds more emunah.

With a little bit of knowledge with regard to physics, we understand that Hashem created electricity and magnetism with positive and negative charges. People seem to have these charges as well. Those with a negative charge find everything worrisome and irritating. They are grouchy and pessimistic and often, their negative energy pushes other people away from them. Nobody wants to come close and be drawn into their world.

On the other hand, some people seem to be charged with positive energy. They don't allow small problems to upset them, and when bigger troubles come along, they are optimistic that Hashem will help. Because they're not wrapped up in their own dark thoughts and feelings, they are more caring and aware of other people. As a result, people are drawn to them. They are the kind of people who make those around them feel good.

Unlike magnets and batteries, people are not created to be negative or positive. Those are traits they create for themselves, and the effort they put into building *emunah* and *bitachon* is the most important factor in determining these traits. When a person is often annoyed with the people in his life and often disappointed at the events in his life, he is not tuned into the belief that Hashem is running the world and doing what is best for him. He hasn't worked on developing his trust in Hashem and therefore, when anything happens that he doesn't like, he feels nothing but his anger. He's like a small child who screams when his father pulls him away from an electrical socket.

Of course, we'd all prefer to be that positively charged person who is beloved by everyone. Someone might think, "That's just not me. It's not my personality. I'm a realistic person and I know that everything doesn't end up in a miracle story." But nobody has to remain stuck with a "negative charge." We can work on ourselves little by little to move into positive territory. It's not even as difficult as we may think, because *emunah* builds *emunah*. Once we stop complaining, our lives somehow present us with fewer and fewer reasons to complain.

The best way to begin making this change is with one small step. Take one area of life that tends to bring out the grouch in you and decide that from now on, you will not complain about it. For instance, if you have a sibling who annoys you, decide that you will just accept that sibling's personality without comment. Or if there's a particular chore or responsibility you tend to complain about, decide that from now on, you'll just do it. You might also choose to make driving in traffic your "no-complaint zone." In all these cases, you can grow your *emunah* by reminding yourself that whatever is happening has come from Hashem; it is as He wants it to be. And what He wants is what is good for you.

Rav Yaakov Yisrael Lugassi tells a story that illustrates how a person can grow in his *emunah* by tackling just one area of his life:

> *There was a man who worked as a sofer, writing sifrei Torah, tefillin, and mezuzos. In such work, there cannot be any mistakes. If there are, then many hours of work can end up being for nothing. This pressure to make each letter perfect made the sofer very tense and anxious. The stress stayed with him even when he was with his family, and as a result, his home was also filled with tension. He felt terrible for his family and for himself as well. He had no place to relax and feel at ease. Something had to change.*
>
> *One day, he took an honest look at his life. "I'm not a tzaddik," he thought. "I'm not the type of person who*

can say 'Gam zu l'tovah' about everything that happens. But in one area of my life — my job — I'm going to stay calm and remind myself that whatever happens is from Hashem."

By practicing this new approach to his work, he was able to overcome the stress he had been feeling. More importantly, by accepting that mistakes might happen and that if so, he will still be able to earn his living, he strengthened his emunah. This carried over into other areas of his life and now, this sofer whose stomach was in knots all day and night is a calm person with a calm home.

MAKE IT REAL:

Choose your own no-complaint zone. Keep track of your efforts by writing down each day for two weeks instances that might have upset you before, but are now being handled with emunah. Do you notice any changes in yourself as a result?

41

When Will I Get Married?

Someone plans it.

Depending on your age, this question may or may not be on your mind. In either case, you can appreciate the enormous extraordinary miracle that's involved in bringing together a couple in marriage. Think of it: Right now, there's someone out there in the world — someone you probably don't even know exists — who will become your partner in life. You will live under the same roof, raise children together, and with Hashem's help, grow old together. For most people, marriage occupies a far greater portion of their years on earth than do their single years.

How does this life-long bond come into being? If we trace the path of a *shidduch*, it seems like a long series of coincidences that are impossible to foresee. But Someone did foresee it. Someone plans it, pushes each partner along the right track, blocks off the wrong tracks, and inspires the right ideas in the right people's minds. Someone puts each partner through certain life experiences that bring him and her to the spiritual level that will be right for the other. Someone orchestrates events in each partner's life to make sure that he or she will develop the personality and *middos* that the other partner needs for optimal growth and accomplishment. Someone — one Someone — does all this just so that a certain boy will meet a certain girl and decide to build a life together.

A *shidduch* is so complex, involving so many intricate steps, that only Hashem can make it happen. The Vilna Gaon tells us, "We must put total trust in Hashem," which means, according to Rav Shlomo Zalman Auerbach, that our part in the process is minimal. A person should contact a few *shadchanim* and let friends and family know that he or she is seeking a *shidduch.* Giving occasional reminders is also considered appropriate. However, beyond that, we must stand back and let Hashem's miracle shine.

When we review the events that lead to the *chuppah*, we see Hashem's hand so clearly that we are filled with overflowing *emunah.* The challenge is to rev up our *emunah* and *bitachon* while we're in the process of finding our match. For some people, this period of life is a long saga. For some, it involves many ups and downs, high hopes and sad disappointments. We cannot know where all this is leading until we get there. We rise to the challenge when we keep ourselves strong, trusting that every seeming detour and roadblock is necessary to make us who we need to be and bring us to the person we are meant to marry.

A *shidduch* is one of Hashem's clearest announcements that He runs the world with love and care for us as He takes us step by step through the maze that leads us to the person he has chosen for us. When a match is meant to be, nothing will stand in its way.

> *The Gerrer Rebbe, the Chiddushei HaRim, was seeking a match for his daughter. The young man suggested to him was a sincere young man but was not a top student in his yeshivah. Nevertheless, the boy found himself on the road, traveling to meet the great Rebbe. He knew that he would be asked to show his proficiency in Gemara, and because the Rebbe's home was a long distance from his own, the young man wisely decided to use the travel time to review what he had been learning. On the road, the Gemara fell into a mud puddle; all but one page was ruined. The young man thought, "It's for the best. All I can do now is review this page until I know it inside-out."*
>
> *He finally arrived at the Chiddushei HaRim's home and met his prospective father-in-law, who asked him*

what Gemara he was learning. The boy replied, "Bava Metzia." Taking out that volume, the Rebbe decided that rather than starting at the beginning, he would pick a random page in the middle and ask his questions on that. Out of the 119 pages that comprise this volume of Gemara, he chose the one page the boy had studied.

The young man became the son-in-law of the Chiddushei HaRim. Although he wasn't among the top bachurim in his yeshivah, he was the bachur Hashem had chosen to marry the Rebbe's daughter. And so it happened, despite the odds.

MAKE IT REAL:

Ask several married people you know to describe how their shidduch occurred. Notice all the hashgachah pratis involved in each and every match.

42

Your Song to Sing

You're the perfect instrument.

Pinchas loved music. He knew a lot about it, too. But there was one question he could never answer: "What's your favorite song?" At a wedding, he loved the pumped-up dance music with a full band. Driving in his car, he enjoyed a mellow Israeli singer accompanied by an acoustic guitar. At a Melaveh Malkah with his friends, he loved a harmonious Carlebach song with dozens of voices singing together.

Each kind of music had something the others didn't. And each was lacking aspects the others had. The Israeli singer's songs would have lost their flavor with a full band or a dozen voices. The wedding band would have flopped miserably with nothing but an acoustic guitar. Each type of music only sounded right with the instruments and voices for which it was created. All the musicians Pinchas enjoy are talented and successful at what they do. None of them wishes for what the others have because they've learned how to make great music with their own equipment.

This is a *mashal* for us to remember when we think we're missing something in life. It's easy to look at what others have and believe that if we, too, had their assets, we'd be doing so much better in life. We might wonder what Hashem expected of us when He sent us into the world so under-equipped.

The reality, however, is that we're each in this world to make our own kind of music, and we are given what we need to perform it in the most perfectly beautiful way. Not only is what we have an essential part of our performance, but also, what we don't have. The Israeli singer's soulful song would be destroyed by the blaring saxophone of the wedding band.

Yocheved's parents became religious in college under the guidance of a campus Chabad Rabbi. She was born at a point when her parents were still finding their way, figuring out where they fit in among the many "brands" of Torah life they saw around them. Little by little, as more children were born, her parents settled into a Brooklyn neighborhood and joined a shul in which the men wore black hats and the women wore sheitels.

By this time, Yocheved was nine years old. Her family had gone from a kiruv shul to a Modern Orthodox shul to a Chabad shul, and ultimately to a mainstream "black-hat" shul, with wardrobe and minhag changes along the way. She envied her friends whose parents had grown up religious. They always knew just what to do. They knew what to wear, what time to show up at a simchah, when to send a gift to the teacher, how to talk to a rebbi, and so much more that seemed to be "some kind of secret code," as her mother would sometimes say. And they had Bubbi and Zaidy, not Grammy and Poppy.

In Yocheved's eyes, Hashem had given her a raw deal. How was she supposed to be a normal girl? How could she get along in school when her mother didn't even know how to read her homework sheet? How could she invite friends over when her house was decorated so oddly, with its big hanging plants and bright, flowered couch? Why couldn't her father look natural in a hat? It never seemed to rest correctly on his head.

One day, as a teen, Yocheved attended a lecture called "Growing up with Baal Teshuvah Parents." Just knowing that such a speech had an audience gave her hope. Maybe she wasn't alone in her misery. The Rabbi who introduced the main speaker said something that changed Yocheved's entire view of her position in life.

"Each soul is planted in the place where Hashem

wants it to be. The root of your avodas Hashem is in that place. You can't succeed by cutting yourself from your root," he said. "If Hashem wanted you to be the son of the Rosh Yeshivah, then that's what you'd be. But He wanted you to have a broader view of life, to understand different types of people and to use these gifts to fulfill your purpose in the world."

When the lecture was over, Yocheved realized that hers was not an easy path, but it was a path to greatness nonetheless.

Like Yocheved, we all have to find the song we're meant to sing. The instruments we need are not out there somewhere, in someone else's possession, but rather, they're in our hands. Once we realize that we have what we need, we can turn our energy toward bringing into the world our perfectly beautiful sound.

MAKE IT REAL:

What do you think is missing from your life? How might that lack actually give you some kind of special strength or advantage?

43

Get Rich

Bless Hashem and He will bless you.

Your great-aunt Baila comes from her *moshav* in Eretz Yisrael to a family wedding. Since your mother has always been one of her favorite nieces, she makes a special effort to come for a visit to your home. And of course, she doesn't come empty-handed. She brings along two huge bags filled with specially chosen presents for each member of your family.

Now imagine that Aunt Baila gives you your gift and you say a quick thanks, put it down unwrapped, and rush off to do something else. In her eyes, this was a gift not worth giving. She took time to select it for you; she even called to ask your mother what you might enjoy receiving. She imagined your pleasure when you opened it up and saw that it was just what you wanted. Instead, you barely acknowledge the gift and don't even take an extra minute to see what is inside. The next time Aunt Baila comes to visit, she won't bother choosing a special gift because it doesn't accomplish her purpose — to bring you pleasure and show her love for you.

We learn that when Hashem gives us His gifts, a similar concept is at work. Everything He gives us carries a message of His love and care. We acknowledge His gifts by reciting a *berachah* with our full attention and a sincere feeling of thankfulness. In *Mishlei* (10:22), Shlomo HaMelech teaches that "it is the blessing of Hashem that enriches." The *sefer*

Mateh Moshe, written by a student of the *Maharshal,* explains that these words refer to reciting *berachos.*

As we think about our future and wonder what career we will pursue, one of the biggest priorities is that our efforts will earn a good *parnassah* for our families. *Mishlei* is telling us that achieving our goal depends on the gratitude we show Hashem for each gift He gives us. The greater our appreciation, the more He sees that we recognize His love and care, the greater our wealth will be.

Rav Raphael Mamo, in his *sefer Shevo V'Achlamah,* tells this true story:

> *A student at Yeshivah Porat Yosef in Yerushalayim left yeshivah to go into business. In just one year, he became very wealthy. The Rosh Yeshivah, Chacham Bentzion Abba Shaul, told his students that the secret to this student's success was that he focused fully on every berachah he said.*
>
> *Ze'ev, a student in the yeshivah, wanted to see for himself. He went to visit his former classmate in his office. "Shalom aleichem!" his friend greeted him warmly. "Sit down and have a cup of tea."*
>
> *Ze'ev sat down and a few moments later, an employee entered carrying one cup of tea.*
>
> *"Aren't you joining me?" Ze'ev asked.*
>
> *"No," he said. "There's too much going on here with the phones ringing and people knocking at the door. I'm afraid that I'd be too distracted to say a proper berachah. I don't eat or drink until I go home. But anyway, what can I do for you? Do you need some financial help?"*
>
> *"You just gave me $100,000," said Ze'ev as he got up to leave. Indeed, he followed his friend's example and was soon a successful businessman himself. One day, Rav Mamo approached him for a donation to help build his new yeshivah. Ze'ev told the Rav the story of his visit with his former classmate from Porat Yosef. "Teach your students to recite berachos properly and I guarantee that your yeshivah will never lack funds."*
>
> *The Rabbi did as Ze'ev suggested. Saying berachos*

with focus became a hallmark of his yeshivah. That year, a man from Haifa named Koby Zayid came with his brother Mordechai to visit the yeshivah. Impressed by what they saw, they pledged money to purchase a new building. Not long after, other donors came forward to renovate the building and turn it into a magnificent heichal, which still stands.

For most people, saying a *berachah* is a habit — a good habit that is the result of years of training throughout childhood. With an investment of perhaps one extra second, we can use that habit to connect with Hashem over and over again throughout the day, to take a moment to "unwrap the gift" He gives us and recognize Who gave it. With that, we bring ourselves far greater rewards in this world and the Next.

MAKE IT REAL:

Visualize what a berachah really means: A ripe peach springs from a wooden branch? Crispy lettuce pops out of dirt? A loaf of soft bread starts as a hard seed in the ground? Put a little dose of amazement into at least one berachah a day.

44

Live a Charmed Life

Hashem gives chein to the humble.

What does the Hebrew word *"chein"* mean? We translate it as "charm," but what is charm? It's the quality that makes someone appealing and likeable to others. We can't always pinpoint what that quality is; it almost seems like something magical. You might know someone who isn't particularly smart or attractive or amusing or talented, but people just like him or her. When that person walks into a room, the mood improves. When that person asks for a favor, people automatically respond, "Sure, no problem."

Very often, people with *chein* are remarkably successful in life. But how does a person access this quality? In truth, it's a gift from Hashem. However, we can do something to earn that gift, and that is to work on the trait of humility — *anivus.* "To those who are humble Hashem will grant *chein,*" says *Mishlei* (3:34).

We learn from many sources that humility is a key to success. *Orchos Tzaddikim* in *Shaar HaAnavah* teaches that Hashem answers a humble person's prayers immediately. That person comes to Hashem with the feeling that, "I'm nothing on my own. Please help me!" and therefore, He helps. The *sefer* also tells us that Hashem rests His *Shechinah* on a humble person; this is because the humble person's heart has plenty of room to let Hashem in. We also know that humility, ironically, is an astonishing power. A person who has been embarrassed but doesn't respond creates for himself an *eis ratzon* — a particularly powerful situation when Hashem accepts our prayers readily and answers them with an open hand.

Humility adds greatly to the value of everything we do. A small mitzvah done with humility is 1,000 times greater than a big mitzvah done with arrogance, the *Orchos Tzaddikim* teaches. Even in our everyday relationships, humility is the key to success and happiness. An arrogant person is repeatedly feeling insulted or slighted because he believes he deserves honor. A humble person, however, doesn't feel this need; he knows that whatever he has is a gift from Hashem and that is the One to Whom the honor should go. The *Tomer Devorah* (Chapter 2) sums it up: "Humility is the best character trait to possess. It opens the doors to acquire all the others."

One of the most damaging effects of arrogance is that it prevents us from improving ourselves. No one can offer any kind of criticism to an arrogant person because his response is always to reject it — often angrily. This means that he will stumble around in life, falling into foreseeable predicaments and avoidable troubles.

We're not born humble. In fact, we're born thinking we are the center of the world. As we become more aware of Hashem and our place among family, friends, and our community, we begin the life-long work of perfecting our traits. We all have areas in which we have a stronger streak of *gaavah* — arrogance — and those are the areas we need to pinpoint and repair. Whether we pride ourselves on our brains, strength, wealth, or beauty, our task is to recognize that none of it is ours; it's all on loan from Hashem.

The reward for working on humility is *chein*. As this old chassidic tale illustrates, *chein* can change everything:

> *A prince commissioned an expert tailor to sew a suit for him. The tailor's pride soared. Surely he was the most talented tailor in the country! He could not speak to anyone without bragging about his commission. He purchased exquisite materials and worked day and night on his creation. However, when he brought it to the prince, the prince's face darkened into a scowl. He*

threw the suit back at the tailor and said, "This is the best you could do? This is atrocious!"

The tailor's spirit was broken. He went to his Rebbe and told him the story. The Rebbe advised him to take the suit home, remove all the stitching, and sew it again in exactly the same manner. The tailor thought this was odd advice, but he followed it. When he finished, he brought the suit once again to the prince, whose face lit up with delight. He paid the tailor a large sum of money and promised to give him more business in the future.

When the tailor returned to the Rebbe to tell the story, he had one question. "How could he hate the suit one day and love the same suit another day?" The Rebbe answered simply, "You sewed the first suit with arrogance. Then your heart was broken and you sewed the second suit with humility. That's why Hashem granted it chein."

MAKE IT REAL:

Do a "gaavah check" on yourself by pinpointing what gets you angry. Then begin working on that area.

45

Praying Is Doing

If we knew what our tefillos were accomplishing, we'd never want to stop praying.

When we need something, we take action. If we have *emunah* and understand that only Hashem can enable our actions to succeed, we also pray. We think these are two separate strategies: doing and praying. The reality, though, is that praying is the most powerful form of doing.

Our prayers make things happen. We need to use each opportunity for prayer as a chance to talk to Hashem about situations that are troubling us and ask for His help in bringing about solutions. The more we do this, the more we will see answered prayers. One prayer that is especially designed for this purpose is *Shema Koleinu* in the *Shemoneh Esrei*. At that time, a person should ask for everything, big or small, that he needs, says the *Yaaros Devash* (*Derush* 1, p.1).

We shouldn't think for a moment that our requests are too petty to bring to the King of kings. Yes, He runs the universe, makes war and peace, heals the sick, and keeps the planets in their orbits. But He also helps you recall the right answers during your history test, reconciles you with a friend who is angry at you, and gets you into the seminary that is best for you. He looks down from His heights, where He sees the entire universe from end to end, and zooms into your heart, your life. The same Hashem Who makes stars explode makes your sister meet her *bashert*.

Just as nothing is too great or difficult for Hashem, nothing is too small for Him either. If we're going out shopping, we should ask Hashem to lead us to the right store where we'll find what we're looking for at a good price. Likewise, we can pray that our team wins the baseball game; that we find something we've lost; that a Chol HaMoed trip works out well — anything our heart desires. When we do this, we become much more aware of Hashem's constant involvement in our life. Instead of thinking, "Finally, I found my lost folder," we realize that "Hashem answered my prayers!" Instead of feeling nothing more than relief from our frustration, we feel our Father's love as He hears us and answers our request. Our whole outlook on life changes when we count up answered prayer after answered prayer. But it won't happen if we don't pray for the things we want and need.

When we live this way, we come to feel that Hashem is our partner in everything we do. The *Shefa Chaim* of Sanz illustrates what this means with the following story of a *tzaddik*:

> *The students of Rav Pinchas Koritzer once heard the Rebbe, at the end of Shemoneh Esrei, speaking in his own words asking Hashem to get his housekeeper to return to working for his family. The students thought that the Rebbe was probably speaking in some type of code, expressing a thought that had a much deeper meaning. Therefore, they asked him, "Rebbe, what were you really asking Hashem?"*
>
> *He told them, "I meant exactly what I said. My wife is getting older and her health is not what it used to be. My housekeeper told us that she's quitting. So I'm asking Hashem for help. Who else should I ask if not my Father, Who always takes care of me?"*

The secret to effective *tefillah* is to know that it always works. We cannot *daven* with the thought that, "It might help and it certainly can't hurt." We have to know that it does help; the only help there is for us in any area of life comes from Heaven. When we pray with that focus, our prayers have true *kavannah,* and even if we don't see an answer right away, our *tefillah* will accomplish great things for us.

MAKE IT REAL:

Every day in Shema Koleinu, insert a request for something that is important to you on that day. Keep a list of how many of your prayers have been answered.

46

The Solution Is on the Stove

Hashem delivers perfect help at the perfect time.

Your family is going out to dinner in honor of your parents' anniversary. They take you to an expensive restaurant and tell you, "Order whatever you want."

Your mouth is already watering as you look at the menu. After much thought, you choose a thick, juicy slice of roast beef with potatoes and vegetables. The waiter comes, your family orders, and you are soon given a basket of soft, warm rolls to keep you occupied while you wait. As you munch on the bread and wait, you realize that it's taking a very long time for your meal to be served.

"I'm starving!" you complain. "When is the food ever going to come?" A while later, as you continue to wait, you say, "This is the worst restaurant ever! At Burger Maven the food is ready in five minutes!" More time goes by as you look at your empty place setting and wonder if you'll ever be fed.

Then the food comes. Your roast beef is cooked to perfection, piping hot and covered with a delicious gravy. It's possibly the best food you've ever eaten. You realize that all your complaining was not warranted. All this time, the chef was creating a masterpiece for you to enjoy.

When we're waiting for Hashem to help us through a difficult situation or give us something we need, our *emunah* is being tested. If we don't realize this, we may react like the person in the scenario above, complaining bitterly about our frustration while all along, the solution is being lovingly prepared for us. Hashem will deliver it only when it's perfect, when the time is right. Our test is to trust that the solution is "on the stove."

How often do we worry and complain about a situation that seems, in the present, to be impossible for us to deal with? Then, sometime later when the situation is resolved, we realize that we worried for no reason. The resolutions might not have been what we wanted, but we're certainly not in exactly the same state. Sometimes, Hashem doesn't fix the problem, but He gives us strength to deal with it. Later, we find that this strength helps us in our lives. For example, a person who grows up in a poor family may pray to be rich and never actually get there. However, he's learned how to save money, how to overcome envy, and how to know the difference between wants and needs. In these ways, he's far ahead of someone who has always gotten everything he's wanted.

Knowing that Hashem is never asleep, never ignoring us but rather, always on the job taking care of our needs, is our best tool for living through the confusing times we are in — the time before the coming of Mashiach. The latest challenge has been the spread of Covid-19, a virus that no one seems to be able to understand. Scientists, doctors, politicians are all in a continual state of confusion about what the virus does, how to stop it from spreading, and how to treat those who are infected with it. People say, "We're tired of it," and pretend it has gone away.

But this, too, is a test. Answers will come when Hashem sends them. Cures will come when Hashem allows us to develop them. It will be over only when He ends it. If we can just do our best to keep ourselves and others healthy, trusting that the solution is "on the stove," we can use this time to grow tremendously in our patience and *emunah,* and even in our humility. We just have to know that there are things we can't know until Hashem reveals them.

MAKE IT REAL:

The next time you want to say that something you're hoping and praying for "never happened," change the sentence to, "I still have hope that it will."

47

Sometimes You See It; Sometimes You Don't

Doing a mitzvah is its own reward.

In the normal way of the world, we'd expect a person to be devastated if he lost $3 million by keeping a mitzvah. We could just hear him thinking, "Hashem! I did what You told me to do and now look! I lost out on so much money!" Worse yet, he might start doubting that Hashem is watching over us at all.

In a book about *emunah,* the stories are often about people who experience miracles and see their troubles wiped away when they turn to Hashem for help. The real heroes of *emunah,* however, are the people who don't see their reward right before their eyes, but never have a flicker of doubt that by serving Hashem, they gain far more than they seem to have lost. Such a person might look around and see others, who don't keep the mitzvos, getting ahead in life, and yet this doesn't shake his *emunah*. He knows that his reward is far greater, even if he has to wait for months or years, or even until *Olam Haba,* to receive it.

David, who deals in rare, expensive jewelry, is just such a man:

A True Story

One of David's many famous customers was Princess Nasrin of Saudi Arabia. One day, the princess's assistant, escorted by several bodyguards, entered David's store. She was shopping for a new piece of jewelry for the princess. David showed her his finest, most elegant pieces and at last, she settled on a few that she thought might suit the princess's taste. She said she would tell the princess about her options and call David back.

After a few calls during the week to clarify information, the assistant told David that the princess would meet him on Friday evening in the lobby of a hotel. The time of the appointment was very close to Shabbos. If the princess was delayed at all, or their negotiations took too long, David would find himself in the midst of a business deal as Shabbos came in. This was not a possibility in his mind — not even a temptation.

Since the princess had no other time available for the meeting, David told her assistant that he would leave the jewels with the hotel manager. She could inspect them and if she wanted to buy them, she could call David to finalize the deal.

That evening, the princess and her assistant walked into the hotel lobby later than they had planned. The princess carefully inspected the beautiful jewels and decided she wanted to buy them. The price David was asking was $3 million.

"Please call the jeweler and tell him that I want to make the purchase," the princess told her assistant.

It was already Shabbos when David noticed his cell phone light up. A quick glance told him that the caller was the princess's assistant. But what could he do? Even with $3 million riding on him answering the call, Shabbos was Shabbos! It rang again a few minutes later and then a few minutes after that. When it rang the next time, it was the princess herself on the caller ID. David stayed strong. No amount of money was worth sacrificing Shabbos.

He hoped that his story would end with a good, "emunah story" ending, such as the princess calling back after Shabbos, making the purchase, and recommending David to all her princess friends because of his great integrity. In fact, David tried to reach the princess's assistant after Shabbos but no one answered his call.

When he went to retrieve his jewelry from the hotel manager, the manager told him, "They loved the jewelry but when you didn't pick up the phone, they said, 'forget it.'"

Even so, David had no doubt that his $3 million loss was not a loss at all. "I know b'emunah sheleimah that I didn't lose a penny by keeping Shabbos. I only gained."

When we do a mitzvah, we can't measure the result. Nowhere on earth is there a way to measure it. We can only trust in the words of Shlomo HaMelech, who taught that he who obeys a commandment will know no evil (*Koheles* 8:5).

MAKE IT REAL:

When you do a mitzvah that's difficult for you, think of it as a challenge like running the marathon. Even if you don't "win a prize," you take pride in getting to the finish line.

48

He's Mine!

Calling Hashem my G-d brings us close to Him.

What's the difference between calling someone "a friend" or calling him "my friend"? Would you rather your parents call you "a child" or "my child"? After a long day at school, are you looking forward to going to "a house" or "my house"? Would you rather talk over a problem in school with "a rebbi" or "my rebbi"?

Think about the impact of the word "my" when we're speaking about the people, places, and objects that are important to us. This two-letter word is so powerful! It instantly changes the subject of our comment from something out there in the world into something to which we are closely connected. It speaks of our personal involvement and emotion. "My" brings our heart into the matter. Even "my problem" is different than "a problem."

Each day, when we say *Adon Olam,* we say the words, "*V'Hu Keili v'Chai Go'ali* — And He is My G-d and my Eternal Redeemer." This is our chance to truly plug into the power of "my" and claim Hashem as our own. He's not just "a G-d" out there in the Heavens running the world from a distance. He's yours. He cares about you and knows you inside out. He doesn't just keep the world spinning; He keeps your heart beating, beat by beat. He is "my Friend" — the One you trust completely; "my Rebbi" — the One Who guides and teaches you; "my Parent" — the One Who gives you all you need to live, completely out of love; and "my Home" — the place where you totally belong. And yet, He is the awesome and eternal King.

When we recognize Hashem's handiwork in our life, our natural response is to feel that personal connection. When the Jewish people sang the *Shiras HaYam* after crossing the *Yam Suf*, they said, "*Zeh Keili* — This is *my* G-d." Rabbi Ephraim Wachsman explained (from *Shem MiShmuel*) that this was the purpose of the miracle. Hashem wanted the Jewish people to know that He is ours.

There is nothing more mysterious and unknowable than Hashem. However, He does not want to be distant from us. Therefore, He let us know that He is our G-d at the *Yam Suf* and keeps letting us know in hundreds of ways each day. We don't have to understand Him to claim Him as our own, to identify ourselves with Him, recognize His love and return it. Just as a small child doesn't have to understand his mother to know who his mother is and that she's *his* mother, we can enjoy a close bond with Hashem just knowing that He is ours.

> *Rav Yosef Breuer, the grandson of Rav Shamshon Raphael Hirsch, once shared an inspiring memory of his grandfather. He remembered watching Rav Hirsch as he recited Adon Olam each morning. He would say each line slowly, with great concentration, and translate as he went along to make sure that he truly absorbed the meaning of the words.*
>
> *When he got to the words "V'Hu Keili v'Chai Go'ali," his excitement rose to a peak. He shouted the words loudly, repeating, "He is my G-d! He is MY G-d! The great, awesome Hashem — He is mine. My Eternal Redeemer!" (as told by Rabbi Wachsman).*

We say *Adon Olam* every morning just as we begin our day. It's not a long or complicated prayer. The words are simple and straightforward, giving us a perfect opportunity to fully focus and connect. By taking a lesson from Rav Hirsch and finding the excitement in having our very own G-d in our life, we can inject ourselves with a powerful dose of *emunah* as the day begins.

MAKE IT REAL:

Make this emphasis on "V'Hu Keili" a part of your davening each day. Think the words, "He's mine!" as you recite the prayer in Hebrew.

49

The Script Is Written

This is what Hashem has planned.

Your camp is playing a baseball game against a neighboring camp. It's a big yearly event and the feeling of rivalry is high. Since your camp has won this game every year for the past four years, you are certain that you'll win again. Your prediction seems accurate as the innings move along and the score is 7 to 3 in your team's favor. Then, in the seventh inning, an outfielder fumbles the ball with bases loaded. The other team scores three times and the gap begins to close. In the eighth inning, your pitcher seems to lose his focus. It's as if he's pitching to little kids, trying to help them hit the ball! But these aren't little kids. In fact, they load the bases once again, hit a homerun and win the game.

"We should have won this!" Everyone on your team is shouting. They harass the outfielder who fumbled the ball and criticize the pitcher for his easy pitches. If not for these players messing up, everyone agrees, the game would have been won and the camp would have retained its champion status.

This outlook, which seems so obvious to the members of the losing team, is actually the opposite of the truth. The players' mistakes did not cause the team to lose. Rather, Hashem had already determined that the team would lose. The players' errors were only His means to bring it about. While the players still need to practice and improve their skills, their performance at this game was just as it was supposed to be. There was no cause for blaming them for the loss.

The events of our lives are like the script of a play that Hashem has written. Each of us plays our role to the best of our ability, trying to do what's right, what's smart, what's kind, what makes us happy. We think that as long as we play our role properly, everything will work out as we planned. Then if it turns out differently, we become angry and confused and look for someone or something to blame. All of this ignores the fact that the script was already written. It could not have turned out differently.

The *Orchos Tzaddikim* teaches that a person who truly believes that Hashem is the cause of everything that happens, and that He only does what is best for us, is always calm and happy. We can learn what this means in real life from one such person, Rabbi Daniel Frisch, a *mekubal* who wrote many *sefarim*. Rav Lugassi tells the story:

> *When Rabbi Frisch came to America to raise money to print his sefarim, he stayed at the home of a well-respected family. While he was there, he dedicated much of his time to continuing his writing. However, due to his poor health, his fingers were swollen and painful, which made writing into a slow, difficult process. Nevertheless, he didn't give up. He stayed up every night until late, working with great dedication on his manuscript.*
>
> *The family hosting Rabbi Frisch was proud to have so great a tzaddik staying right under their own roof. One night, one of the young men of the family decided to take advantage of the opportunity to hear the Rabbi's wisdom. He went to his room to ask him some questions, and the Rabbi graciously paused his work to speak to his visitor.*
>
> *That's when the unthinkable happened. The young man accidentally knocked over a cup of grape juice that the Rabbi had been drinking and it spilled all over the manuscripts, destroying many hours of work. "I'm so sorry, Rabbi!" the young man said, his voice shaking. "Please forgive me!"*
>
> *"You're asking me for forgiveness, but there's something you need to know," said the Rabbi. "Many years before*

I was born...Hashem in His infinite wisdom wrote down what is going to happen to every single person who would ever live. Of course, things could be changed, but there is a plan for every person according to his soul's needs. Hashem wrote down that on this day, at this time, the writings of a Jew named Daniel Frisch will have juice spilled on them. What could possibly be bad about Hashem's plan for me?"

When we realize that everything is as it should be, we can say goodbye to anger. Nobody does anything to us; we are all simply playing our assigned roles in Hashem's amazing script for His world.

MAKE IT REAL:

The next time something good happens, think, "Oh, this is what Hashem was planning all along." Then do the same when something disappointing happens.

50

A Modified Test

Hashem's tests are designed for success.

Although Leah was already in ninth grade, Hebrew was still difficult for her to read and understand. For that reason, her Chumash tests and Navi tests didn't show what she really knew. In fact, she was an intelligent girl who listened intently and participated in the class discussions. However, when she saw a test paper covered with questions in Hebrew, she felt as if she had never seen the material before. Her Cs and Ds were depressing for her, especially because they were always accompanied by notes from the teacher saying, "You can do better" or "Please spend more time studying."

After one disastrous test, Leah approached her Chumash teacher. "I know this stuff!" she said. "I just get overwhelmed with the Hebrew. I study and study, but when I see it on the test, it flies out of my head. It's very hard for me."

The teacher decided to give Leah a different test than she gave the rest of the class. Leah's test was very hard, but it was in English. As long as she understood what the Chumash and commentators were saying, she could pass it. And she did, with flying colors! Suddenly Leah went from a C-student to an A-student, all because the test was designed for her abilities.

Like this teacher, Hashem designs our tests to challenge us at our level. The Rebbe of Kotzk once said that Hashem never gives a person a test that he is not capable of passing. On the other hand, He doesn't let us just slide by. Rather, He gives us challenges that demand our maximum effort. If we keep in mind that Hashem knows we can do it, we can prevent ourselves from becoming hopeless and thinking, "I just can't..."

Sometimes, Hashem brings us step-by-step into a situation that would seem overwhelming if it came upon us all at once. For example, a newlywed woman sees a young mother walking through the aisles of a grocery store with a baby in the seat of the cart, another child riding inside the cart, and two others hanging onto the sides. The baby is crying and one of the children is begging for a snack. The newlywed thinks, "I could *never* do this! I'd go out of my mind! I don't have that kind of patience." Fortunately, however, Hashem usually gives parents one child at a time. As the family grows, the parents become emotionally stronger, more mature, and more capable. While the mother at the grocery store might have been struggling to maintain her cool and get her errands done, it was a test she could pass.

We learn this idea from the Torah, when Hashem commands Avraham to bring Yitzchak as an offering. First, Hashem says, "Take, please, your son" (*Bereishis* 22:2). Since Avraham had two sons, he asked, "Which one?" To this, Hashem said, "your only son," but Avraham had two "only sons," one from Sarah and one from Hagar. Therefore, Hashem led him to the next step, "the one you love." Avraham loved them both. Finally, Hashem specified: "Yitzchak."

With each step, says Rav Chaim Shmulevitz, Hashem eased Avraham into this historic test. In this way, He gave Avraham the greatest chance to succeed. Why, then, didn't He make it even easier, asks Rav Lugassi. Why didn't Hashem tell Avraham, "I love you so much. I would only tell you to do something that is good for you." The reason is that the four steps with which Hashem led Avraham to understand what he was being asked to do were enough. Had Hashem made the test easier, the merit for it would have been less. He would have scored a 95 instead of a 100. The Jewish people would be missing a major portion of the *zechus Avos* — the merit of the Forefathers — that has protected us throughout our history.

Sometimes, we fool ourselves into thinking we don't have the ability to pass our tests. It may be because peer pressure is pulling us in the wrong direction and we don't realize we have the power to resist it. It might also be because our belief in Hashem is shaky; we feel that "If I only *knew* Hashem is here, I'd be able to do the right thing." That's when we have to remind ourselves of two important points: First, if we couldn't pass the test, Hashem wouldn't put it in our lives; and secondly, we can only gain by giving it all we've got.

MAKE IT REAL:

Is there something in your life that seems to be too much for you? Try to break it down into smaller steps. Then remind yourself that if Hashem is asking this of you, He's already given you the strength to do it.

51

Wise Words Are Never Wasted

Keep learning and change will come.

People do a lot of talking. Much of it is practical: we are just giving or receiving information to keep our life running smoothly. Some talk is entertaining, like a funny story or a good joke.

However, because our power of speech is the part of us that is most closely tied to our *neshamah,* we know it has much loftier roles to fill. Speech is the ability that allows us to talk to Hashem through *tefillah* and to learn how to serve Him through our Torah learning. In addition, words can convey ideas that change our or another person's life.

Imagine that you know someone who is heading in the wrong direction. If this is someone you care about, such as a friend or sibling, you might try to wake him up and get him to change his path. You might tell him your most inspiring story or make your most logical argument. Sadly, however, it sometimes seems that our words float off into outer space, never reaching their target. Our words seem wasted.

Sometimes, the person we need to inspire is ourself. We read about *emunah,* listen to *shiurim,* and try so hard to bring the words into our heart. Then we wonder, why isn't it sticking? Why do we seem to have the same fears, the same worries, the same resentments as we've always had? Are these words of *emunah* and encouragement wasted? Should we just give up on ourselves and other people because nothing seems to change?

The fact is that positive words are never wasted. They will have an impact, but it may come in weeks, months, or even years. Words might be compared to the water flowing over rock. Eventually, the water will wear a groove in the rock — but it will take many years. Until we see that groove, we will find it hard to believe that water has the power to change the shape of solid rock.

Likewise, you might point out to someone who is feeling down, "Wow! Hashem loves you!" and mention some accomplishment he's recently achieved or some item he's recently purchased. He may have a thousand proofs as to why Hashem *doesn't* seem to love him, but you've at least turned his focus in the other direction for a few minutes. If you do that every so often, he might begin to see it himself. And if not now, then maybe five years from now; something wonderful will happen and he'll think, "Wow! Hashem loves me!"

Rabbi Yoel Gold told a story that shows us how real the impact of words can be:

> *When Lisa* was 12, she used to babysit for her neighbor's children. Although the children were part of a secular family, Lisa said Shema Yisrael with them when she put them to bed. That was their entire Jewish education.*
>
> *About 20 years later, one of these children, a boy named Jordan, was fighting with the U.S. Army in the Iraq War. Whenever he felt alone or frightened, he remembered the words "Shema Yisrael" and said them with all his heart. He felt that this saved him from danger.*
>
> *After the war, Jordan decided to go to Israel and learn more about Judaism. He joined Yeshivas Ohr Somayach. One day, he told a new friend in yeshivah about his babysitter and how her "Shema" helped him in the war. The friend, who was from the same city, asked him, "Do you remember the babysitter's name?" Jordan told him the name.*
>
> *"That's my sister!" said the friend. He called her right away to let her know that her Shema had achieved far more than she had ever imagined.*

Whether we're trying to build our own *emunah* or encourage someone else, we should always believe that words have power. The more we learn and speak about *emunah*, the sooner we'll see what it can really do.

MAKE IT REAL:

Whether from a book or a shiur, keep words of emunah flowing into your life day by day.

52

Just Plain Annoying

Emunah is never a waste of time.

We think of *emunah* as the belief that whatever happens is from Hashem, and therefore is for our good. Naturally, we expect to eventually see the good. That's why we gain so much strength from stories in which someone loses out, accepts the loss as Hashem's will and soon finds that He had something better in store for him. In these cases, we can clearly see that the person's *emunah* is rewarded.

An even greater level of *emunah* is available to us in situations that don't reveal any big, happy ending. Sometimes we made a big effort only to find that our time was wasted. For example, you spend several nights studying for an exam. The night before the exam, you review everything — a whole term's worth of material — to make sure it's all fresh in your mind for the next morning. You get to school and find out that the teacher has had an emergency and a substitute will be finishing out the school year. And guess what — the exam has been canceled.

This type of situation doesn't have the drama and challenge of a real *nisayon* like an illness or a loss. In such cases, our hearts are open; we pray for and receive Hashem's comfort. Neither does an annoyance have the wonderful sense of "Aha! Look how Hashem made it all work out for me in the end!" It's just an annoyance. It's hard to be anything but annoyed.

We all know the story of Rabbi Akiva, who stopped along his route to seek shelter overnight in a town. When he was refused shelter, he camped out in a field with his donkey, a candle by which to learn, and a rooster to awaken him. As each of these was taken from him by various misfortunes, he said, "Everything Hashem does is for the best." The next day, he discovered that bandits had invaded the town and captured the townspeople. If not for their refusal to take him in, he'd have been captured. If not for the loss of the candle, rooster, and donkey, the bandits would have found him. He saw how his "misfortunes" protected him.

Now let's ask ourselves — how good a story would this be if the town had not been attacked — if Rabbi Akiva had simply lost a night of learning, overslept, and been forced to continue his trip on foot? It might have been less of a testimony to Hashem's *hashgachah pratis* but more of a testimony to Rabbi Akiva's *emunah*.

Simple irritations of life call for simple faith. We truly don't know why such things happen. We can't see any spiritual or practical gain from them. Still, we have to remind ourselves that even this is from Hashem. Our job under these circumstances is to calm ourselves down, wipe away our anger at those who "caused" us to waste our time, and realize that this time was meant to be wasted for reasons we may never know.

A True Story

During the peak of the coronavirus in the spring of 2020, Mendy bought a new car. However, because all businesses and offices were closed, he couldn't go to the New Jersey Motor Vehicle Commission to register it. At last, on a hot summer day, the MVC reopened. Expecting long lines, Mendy arrived at 7:30 a.m., an hour before opening time. The line already stretched across the parking lot. Having only a few days available to take care of this chore, he decided to stick it out no matter how long it took.

At 4 p.m., the office announced that it was closing. Mendy was eighth from the front of the line. Each person was given a number and assured that they would be taken in that order the next day. Therefore, the next morning, Mendy went back to the MVC and within a short while, he was inside showing his documents to the clerk.

"I'm sorry, sir," said the clerk, "but this type of registration has to be done by our main office in Trenton." Nine hours in the hot sun, plus a return trip that morning, had all been for nothing.

When Mendy returned home, his wife and children were appalled on his behalf. "It's crazy! You wasted a whole day! Poor Daddy!" they sympathized. But Mendy was unfazed. "It is what it is — it's what Hashem wanted," he said. "I tried to get it done and it didn't work out. Worse things can happen."

When we call upon our *emunah* to help us through situations that might seem meaningless, we give extraordinary meaning to the moment. It becomes an opportunity to strengthen our belief that everything — even an annoyance — has a reason, and to accept Hashem's will calmly and quietly.

MAKE IT REAL:

Look forward to your next annoyance! Use it as a chance to say, "I don't know what the good of this is, but it's what Hashem wanted."

53

Who You Know

It's not the hishtadlus that decides the result.

"It's not what you know, it's who you know." This is an old saying that expresses a belief that even many Torah Jews hold, which is that a person's success depends on making connections with powerful, influential people. This means that if you want to get into a particular yeshivah, you need to find a big donor or someone who knows the *menahel* to speak on your behalf. If you want to get rich, you have to make rich friends. If you're sick, you need to get an appointment with the best doctor. If you want to get married, you need to "get on the radar" of the biggest *shadchanim*.

When we make these efforts with the right ideas in our mind, they fall under the category of *hishtadlus* — the practical efforts we are required to make in order to give Hashem a natural means to fulfill our needs. Our own effort is a necessary part of the process. For example, if we don't open our mouth to eat, Hashem won't feed us. If we don't open a *sefer* to learn, He won't fill our minds with knowledge. Even *Gedolim* tell us that if a person is sick, he should seek the best doctor to treat his condition. There is nothing wrong with doing this.

However, when we think that our success *depends* on "who we know," we are not making *hishtadlus*; we are turning that person into Hashem. We're allowing ourselves to see another human being as the one who determines what will happen to us. This is a mistake.

First of all, it's completely untrue. If a certain yeshivah is where Hashem has decided we should be learning, no one can deny us our place. The person we're counting on to "pull strings" may not help us, but someone will. Similarly, we will meet our *bashert*, whether through the world's most sought-after *shadchan* or through a friend our mother meets in the supermarket.

Secondly, when we believe our fate rests in another human being's hands, we may become angry or hopeless if the person refuses. Instead, we have to realize that if Hashem wants our effort to succeed, He can choose from the entire population of the world to find a messenger to help us.

The *Chovos HaLevavos* teaches that a person with true *emunah* knows that every person is equally likely to be the one who helps him. Just because someone has more to offer doesn't mean he will offer it. A billionaire might refuse a person a $5,000 loan, but another person who is nowhere near as wealthy might have a *ma'aser* fund from which he happily and easily makes the loan.

With all this in mind, we can do our *hishtadlus* and seek help from those we believe can help us. However, we must always remember that the help is coming from Above. If it's meant to come, it will — if not from one person, then from another.

A True Story

When Batsheva's mother received a call from a renowned shadchan, she felt that she had struck gold. The shadchan had a wealthy client who had heard of Batsheva. The shadchan wanted to send the boy's resume.*

The mother was amazed at this unexpected development. Her daughter had wanted to marry a learning boy, but the family lacked the means to provide support. Here was a family that wasn't looking for support, didn't need support, with a son who wanted to remain in learning and then join his father's successful business. And they were seeking her out!

After making her inquiries, the mother gave an OK. The couple went out and things went very well. Then, before the expected seventh date, the boy dropped out, no reason given.

"Don't worry," the shadchan told Batsheva. "I have a lot of other boys that are good possibilities for you." Despite her deep disappointment, Batsheva felt that with this shadchan's help, she was sure to bounce back quickly. However, weeks went by, reminder texts were sent, but no new suggestions were forthcoming. Once again, she gave up on her hope of marrying a learning boy and tried to focus on her job, her friends, and her personal growth.

One day about a year later, her brother called her. What would she think of going out with his friend's younger brother? He had just started dating, and the friend thought it might be a match. Within a month, Batsheva and this boy were engaged. He was learning full-time and happy to live on the money Batsheva earned, his kollel stipend, and a small monthly contribution from Batsheva's family. The big shadchan didn't make the match, but the Biggest Shadchan did.

MAKE IT REAL:

If you find yourself becoming obsessed about "getting in" with certain people whom you believe can help you, remind yourself that Hashem's help can come through anyone.

54

Tefillah Is REAL!

Prayers make things happen.

When we have a problem, we think there are two ways to handle it: we can do something real and practical and also, we can pray. We don't often look at our prayers as a real and practical effort to bring about the solution to our problem. In dire situations, when there seems to be nothing any human being can do to help, people might say, "All we can do now is pray," as if this is a last-ditch strategy to be used when there's nothing left to lose.

This idea of prayer misses the point. Prayer *is* the answer. It is the most practical of all strategies, because it's the only thing that really works. We have no idea what power our prayers hold. The Chofetz Chaim tells us that Hashem has more pleasure from the praises of one single Jew than from the praise of all the Heavenly angels combined. He created us for the very purpose of connecting to Him and bringing His light into the world, and prayer is the cord that connects us.

When we pray with our heart, focusing on the words and their meaning, we can feel Hashem's embrace. The *Midrash* comments that the words of *Shir HaShirim* (8:3), "His right arm embraces me," refer to prayer. When we pray, we are running into our Father's loving arms, deriving strength and comfort through our connection. But prayer doesn't only make us feel better; it makes our situation better, because we are calling upon the only One Who can help.

The effect of prayer is so real that the Chofetz Chaim says we are performing an actual *chesed* when we pray for others in need of Hashem's help. Of course, we should also do all we can to alleviate others' difficulties in practical ways, but our prayers for them are no less valuable. In fact, the Chofetz Chaim teaches that when a person leaves this world, he might discover that he has exceptional merit for all the good that happened as a result of his prayers. For example, imagine that you know someone who is heading off the path of Torah. You pray for him to return and eventually, he does. You might not realize that all the mitzvos he performs throughout his life are bringing you merit. Or perhaps you pray for someone who is ill. You might not realize that you are credited with saving a life!

A True Story

A man from California had to go to Eretz Yisrael on business. It was 2015, about a year after the Gaza War. The man's wife decided to join him on the trip, and they followed a friend's advice to eat at a certain restaurant in Herzliya.

Once they were seated at the restaurant, the woman decided that she'd rather sit on the second floor where the lighting was better. They moved upstairs and their waiter came to give them menus and tell them about the specials of the day. "My name is Barak," he told them. "I'll be back soon to take your order."

"I wonder if his mother's name is Orna," the wife said to her husband. "Last summer, during the Gaza war, I called a hotline to get the name of a soldier to pray for. I was given the name Barak ben Orna, and I've had his name posted on the kitchen cabinet this entire year. I still pray that he should be safe, and lately, I've been wondering what became of him. I asked Hashem to let me know if he was still alive."

When the waiter returned, the woman asked him if his mother's name was Orna. With a surprised expression, he answered that it was. "How did you know?" he asked.

"Your name is on my kitchen cabinet," the woman explained. "I've been praying for you to come home safely. I'm so happy to see you!"

Tears filled the soldier's eyes. "Someone was praying for me to come home safely, and I did! Thank you!" he said.

The woman realized that Hashem was listening to her relatively small request for information on the soldier. He led her to this restaurant and even caused her to change her seat so that Barak would be her waiter. The soldier realized that there is a G-d in Heaven and began putting on tefillin the next day.

Tefillah isn't a "just in case" or "it can't do any harm" strategy. It's the greatest power Hashem has given any of His creations. It gives us a hand on the steering wheel that moves the world.

MAKE IT REAL:

Take one need in your life — whether your own or that of a friend or family member — and think as you're praying for it that "I'm taking the best step toward getting it done."

55

Follow Me!

We can't get lost when we follow Hashem.

Imagine: A war is going on. Bombs are dropping all over the city. You and your family are huddled together with others in a bomb shelter. Suddenly a man enters the shelter and says, "This isn't a safe place to stay. Everyone follow me. I'll take you to safety." This man is someone everyone trusts. He's wise and resourceful and he knows every street, tunnel, and alleyway in the city. They willingly line up behind the man, hold on to him and follow him to wherever he will take them. They're not afraid.

When we show this kind of trust and reliance on Hashem, it is the ultimate show of our love. He never forgets these moments, and they are among our greatest sources of merit. *Yirmiyahu* (2:2) quotes Hashem's words, "I recall for you the lovingkindness of your youth, the love of your bridal days, your following Me into the Wilderness, in an unsown land." How could He not be moved by such faith? We didn't know where we were going, what we would eat, how we would live, and yet we followed Hashem. The Jewish people were like a young bride who follows her husband into an unknown future. Who knows what lies ahead? Only her trust in the man she is marrying gives her the courage to make such a leap. In reality, however, this all stems from trust in Hashem, because He is the One Who brought her this husband and He is the One Who will map out the path of their life together.

This deep trust goes back even further in Jewish history, to the very beginning when Avraham heard Hashem's command, "*Lech lecha*" — directing him to leave his homeland and family for an unknown destination that Hashem would show him. Throughout the Torah, our ancestors' comings and goings were all directed by Hashem's word. After they left Mitzrayim, they continued following Hashem as He commanded them to travel and to encamp during their 40 years in the Wilderness.

In our own lives, we can still express this loving trust, and merit the great rewards that come with it. We do this when we make our best effort to follow the path Hashem lays out for us — to do what is right, even when it's hard, even when it seems we might be happier if we take a shortcut or avoid a strenuous effort. In such cases, our job is to shut off our doubting voice, rev up our courage and energy and say, "Hashem won't steer me wrong!"

> *A scenario: Many of Moshe's friends were getting married. Moshe, however, was in no hurry. He was enjoying his life and his freedom. Yeshivah was going well and even with a full learning schedule, he still had some time to travel and go camping with his friends. He couldn't imagine being one of those guys who answered, "Let me check with my wife" before he could agree to go out for a hamburger or play a game of basketball.*
>
> *By the time Moshe was 23, his disinterest in marriage had grown. Now his friends were mixing baby formula and pushing strollers and leaving weddings early because "the babysitter can only stay until 10." Nevertheless, he finally gave in to the constant pressure to start dating. After all, he reasoned, it could still take another year or more to actually get married.*
>
> *He hadn't counted on meeting Rivka. As they began getting to know each other, his vision of life began to change. After several deep conversations with his rebbi, he began to realize that, difficult as it all seemed, marriage and family were the path Hashem had created to achieve a meaningful life, and most importantly, Hashem would be with him all the way. The day he became engaged to*

Rivka, he felt like a diver who had climbed to the highest cliff and was now staring down into the river below. "I'm going to jump, Hashem, and You're going to catch me," he thought. "Here goes!"

It was a thrilling jump and a safe, happy landing. Moshe knew that life would require many more daring dives into the unknown, but he now knew that he wouldn't have to do it alone.

MAKE IT REAL:

If there is a situation that you are trying to avoid, give yourself courage to take the first step in the right direction, knowing that Hashem is leading the way.

56

Your Amazing Miracle Machine

Being grateful for our health brings great health.

Never does a person think, "Wow, it's such a gift to have a healthy pinky toe!" Toes are among those things that are meant to function quietly, without drawing any attention to themselves. However, if you happen to be walking barefoot in your room and you accidentally bash your pinky toe into a heavy object lying on the floor — let's say a 20-pound weight you forgot to put away — that toe will be speaking to you for days. Your shoe won't fit on your foot. Your toe will ache. You won't be able to stand or walk for long. Suddenly, the only thing on your mind will be your pinky toe. When it finally feels better, you'll be so grateful to be able to walk normally again.

We see then that even our smallest toe has a significant effect on our ability to function. How much more so, then, do we count on the millions of far more intricate processes that take place in our body so silently and efficiently that we don't even know they're happening. Think about it: If our blood clotted within our veins, we'd die. If it didn't clot when it oozed out of a cut or a wound, we would also die. What makes it clot? The process is a complicated dance involving various proteins, blood vessels narrowing themselves to slow the bleeding, and blood cells changing shape to link together and form a mesh over the cut. That's what has to happen for your little brother's scraped knee to form a scab. When it works, we don't think about it. When it doesn't work, we can't think about anything else.

The design of our body is so clear a proof that Hashem, in His infinite wisdom, designed the world, that if we would only focus on it from time to time, we would never have a doubt. However, our physical processes are barely noticeable to us, and that's as Hashem meant it to be. We would get very little done in life if our attention was riveted on our inhales and exhales, swallows and blinks.

Nevertheless, there is one occasion in our day when we are commanded to focus on the wonder of our body and thank our Creator for His miraculous creation. That is when we say *Asher Yatzar* after taking care of our needs. Unlike other functions such as our heartbeat and breathing, our digestion is a process that has a beginning, middle, and completion. In the midst of the process, our body is releasing dozens of different enzymes and chemicals, our blood is absorbing various nutrients as the food breaks down, an entire world of bacteria is converting the food into usable nutrients, muscles are moving the food along 15 feet of intestine and finally, the waste products leave our body. The life-sustaining digestive process comes to its completion and at that point, we stop and thank Hashem.

Saying this *berachah* with *kavannah* is known to have the power to cure illness. It has been recommended by countless *Gedolim,* including Rav Meir of Premishlan and the Chofetz Chaim. But even in perfect health, when we stop for a few moments in our day to thank Hashem for the great gift of a healthy, functioning body, the Gift-giver only wants to give us more.

A True Story

A tiny baby came into the world with a rare health problem that prevented his blood from absorbing glucose, the sugar that provides energy to the brain and body. After a surgery to remove most of his pancreas, and many months in the hospital, he was finally stable enough to go home. Still, he needed round-the-clock medications, some so powerful that even a tiny extra droplet could be lethal.

As he grew, many new problems emerged. He wasn't

able to eat like a normal child, and so his mother spent a summer at a special program that offered feeding therapy. All throughout his younger years, he needed constant supervision to make sure that he ate enough to keep his blood sugar at a healthy level. So many "normal" functions in this boy's life were only achieved with effort.

"We really see the chochmah in Asher Yatzar," the boy's mother once said. "Because all these problems come from things that are not opening and closing correctly. It's on a micro-level, but really that's at the bottom of it."

Throughout the early years of this challenge, the parents' friends and family said "Asher Yatzar" with this boy in mind. And little by little, this child from whom doctors expected nothing but setbacks and troubles, became healthy and strong, even serving in the IDF. Today he is a young married man looking forward to a bright future.

MAKE IT REAL:

Protect your health by appreciating it. At least once a day, make sure to say Asher Yatzar with full concentration on the miracle of a healthy, functioning body.

57

There's No Doubt About It

The Torah proves that Hashem exists.

Imagine that 3,000 years ago, a man told his family a story about how the world came into being. As part of the story, he created a long list of rules that he wanted his family to live by and told them that these rules came from the invisible being that created the world. How likely do you think it would be that 3,000 years later, after this family has expanded to include millions of people and has spread out all over the world, that they would still be studying that story day after day and living by the rules their long-ago ancestor set forth for them?

The answer is that it is not likely at all. Times change, people change, beliefs change, and a way of life that made sense 3,000 years ago would seem irrelevant today. Now, let's add to the scenario the fact that the rest of the world tries its best to stop this family from keeping to their way of life. Entire nations rise against them with weapons, restrictions, and persecution of all sorts. How long would it take for this family to give up their fight? Two generations? Three?

When we look at this scenario, we see what an entirely unnatural, miraculous phenomenon the Jewish nation is. That alone gives us strong proof that the Torah comes from Hashem and that we are the nation He chose to bring His holiness into the world by doing His mitzvos. What else could keep us going so long and so strong? What else could enable us to survive so much adversity?

But it's not just the facts of history that bear out the truth of the Torah. It's the Torah itself. It provides information about matters that only Hashem could know, because only He knows all of human history from its beginning to its end. Therefore, the Torah can "safely" say, "Go and search history from the beginning of Creation until today and you will find that no other nation ever claimed to hear G-d speaking to them together, as Hashem spoke to us on Sinai" (see *Devarim* 4:32). The Torah's "today" is not the "today" on which Moshe addressed the Jewish people, but rather, the "today" of all the generations. Indeed, his words are as true today as they were when he spoke them. But only Hashem could know that from the approximately 4,000 religions that would develop in the world, none would ever claim to have experienced a Divine revelation before an entire nation.

The Torah includes many other "only Hashem could have known" facts as well. When Hashem commands the Jews to leave their homes and travel to Yerushalayim for the *Shalosh Regalim,* it promises that "No one will covet your land" in their absence. How could the Torah promise that there would be no invaders or intruders when thousands of homes were left vacant? If just one home was robbed, the truth of the Torah would be disproven.

Similarly, the Torah promises that the land will produce enough food for three years in the year prior to *Shemittah.* No one could fail to realize if the Torah's prediction didn't materialize. Indeed, Eretz Yisrael's farmers still observe *shemittah,* and with greater participation in each new cycle. The Torah's statements can only be made by the One Who controls everything.

Do we need these proofs to believe in Hashem? Obviously, Hashem knows that we do. Doubts are natural, especially when we are trying to connect to the spiritual world that is invisible to our eyes. However, if anyone wants to believe, he doesn't have to unravel complicated Kabbalah concepts. He just has to look at what's right in front of him — a Torah and a Jewish nation that can only have come from Hashem.

The American writer, Mark Twain, once wrote these lines regarding the Jewish people:

The Egyptian, the Babylonian, and the Persian rose, filled the planet with sound and splendor, then faded to dream-stuff and passed away; the Greek and the Roman followed, and made a vast noise, and they are gone; other peoples have sprung up and held their torch high for a time, but it burned out, and they sit in twilight now, or have vanished. The Jew saw them all, beat them all, and is now what he always was, exhibiting no decadence, no infirmities of age, no weakening of his parts, no slowing of his energies, no dulling of his alert and aggressive mind. All things are mortal but the Jew; all other forces pass, but he remains. What is the secret of his immortality?

Mark Twain saw what many Jews, themselves, do not see, which is our miraculous survival throughout the centuries. However, his question, "What is the secret?" is no mystery to us. We are eternal because of Hashem and the Torah He gave us.

MAKE IT REAL:

When you say in Aleinu the words, "v'yadata hayom v'hasheivosa el levavecha ki Hashem Hu haElokim..." (and you know this day and take into your heart that Hashem, He is G-d), think of some of the facts above.

58

Yours Is the Gift He Wants

Hashem treasures every small thing we do for Him.

It's your mother's birthday tomorrow. Before bedtime, your six-year-old sister takes out her paper, markers, and glue and begins working on a birthday card. The pictures are basically stick figures. The writing is backwards, and the spelling is creative, but somehow, she manages to draw herself and your mother holding hands, and to write something that looks enough like "Happy Birthday Mommy." But that's only a card. She wants to give Mommy a present as well, so she opens her knapsack and takes out a lollypop and a taffy she had gotten on Friday at her class Shabbos party. These she tapes to the card. She goes to bed satisfied. Tomorrow morning, she'll sneak into the kitchen early and put the card and gift on the table so that Mommy will see it when she comes down for her coffee.

Imagine the feeling this mother will have when she sees her little girl's offering. It's such a small thing, but it's her daughter's best effort, given with pure love. No matter how small and insignificant this gift is in the objective sense, it means the world to the mother.

Now let's think about our capacity to "give" anything to Hashem. What is it worth? What can even the greatest human being do that would be of value to Him? This feeling that our efforts have very little value causes a wall to rise up between us and Hashem. Our only way of connecting to Hashem is through prayer, Torah learning, and mitzvos, and if we feel that these activities are meaningless to Him, why would we pursue them? We would rather think, "He exists in His world and I live in mine."

That's why we absolutely must realize how precious every small effort is. The *Chovos HaLevavos* (*Shaar Cheshbon HaNefesh*) writes, "A person should not underestimate even the smallest thing he does for Hashem. What we think is small, is great in His eyes."

The Torah teaches us this lesson through the lights of the Menorah in the Beis HaMikdash. Why are we lighting these small oil lamps for Hashem, Who has all the light in the universe? It's like giving pennies to a billionaire! But the *Midrash* (*Parashas Behaaloscha*) teaches that Hashem, out of His incredible love for us, says, "All the light I have is nothing compared to yours. I only want to use your light."

How touching and beautiful it is to think of ourselves as Hashem's precious children whose gifts, small and insignificant as they may be, are so delightful to Him. Like the mother in our opening scenario, He treasures the efforts that come from our heart and represent our desire to please Him. Our *avodas Hashem* is always worthwhile, no matter how little, how late, how flawed. He doesn't need our light, but He loves it.

BASED ON A TRUE STORY

Robert's past few weeks had been very unusual for him. Through a friend at work, he had begun to be interested in Judaism. He went to shul for the first time ever on the Shabbos before Shabbos HaGadol. He loved the atmosphere and found the Rabbi's speech about the upcoming holiday of Pesach to be very inspiring. He was happy to discover that he hadn't forgotten the Hebrew he had learned in his Conservative Hebrew school as a child.

Now, it was a Tuesday night and he was sitting with some friends at a non-kosher restaurant. It was also Chol HaMoed Pesach. The friends weren't religious — some weren't even Jewish. The waiter put a basket of warm garlic bread on the table and the aroma drifted pleasantly into Robert's nostrils. The friends all helped themselves to the soft, steaming pieces of bread, but Robert held back. "Nah, I'm not going to eat a piece of bread on Pesach," he thought to himself.

The meal came and he ate it. Surely it was as far from kosher l'Pesach as a meal could be. Did his little gesture of skipping the bread mean anything when he ate a plate of breaded fried (tereifah) chicken? Many years later, when he was already fully Torah observant, he thought about that very question and answered it himself. "That was the first thing I ever did in my life that was l'sheim Shamayim. Hashem loved it!"

Rather than thinking of himself as a hypocrite who refrained from eating the bread but ate a meal that was both *tereifah* and *chametz,* Robert felt good about refraining from the bread. He had done something just for Hashem, and he felt in his heart that Hashem recognized it.

MAKE IT REAL:

Don't let your small efforts pass unnoticed. Say to yourself as you make an effort in your avodas Hashem, "Hashem, this is for You!"

59

What I Need to Do Now

Hashem will show you what your job is.

Avraham Avinu knew what Hashem wanted from him. Avraham was supposed to teach the world about Hashem and His kindness. He was supposed to turn people away from cruel, false gods that they served by sacrificing their children. Most importantly, he was supposed to teach his household, especially his son Yitzchak, to carry on the ways of Hashem.

Then one day, Hashem told Avraham to take his son Yitzchak and bring him as an offering. Now what? Avraham was stuck between the mission Hashem had given him and the request Hashem was now making. As the *Lev Eliyahu* (*Parashas Lech Lecha*) explains, by sacrificing Yitzchak, Avraham would be contradicting everything he stood for. Nevertheless, without any hesitation, he followed Hashem's will as He expressed it at that moment. Hashem had shown Him what He wanted, and Avraham was a faithful servant who did as he was asked.

This approach to our *avodas Hashem* can help us become flexible and calm when it seems to us that Hashem Himself is standing in the way of our spiritual success. We may think, "I want to do this mitzvah. I want to do it right. Why is Hashem putting obstacles in my way?" If we think like Avraham, however, we will look at the situation in which Hashem puts us and think, "This is how He wants me to serve Him right now."

This situation arises far more often than we can imagine,

because we are rarely surrounded by the perfect conditions for performing a mitzvah. For example, a student wants to spend several hours carefully reviewing his learning. He pictures himself sitting in a quiet room focused on his *sefer,* his mind completely absorbed. However, his grandfather has a medical emergency; his mother must run to the hospital and his father is away on business. He's now in charge of the house, which means getting four small children to bed. Should he say, "How am I supposed to learn Torah when I have to take care of a bunch of little kids?"

No! If he follows Avraham Avinu's lead, he will instead say, "Hashem has given me this job to do," and he will do it with the same focus and enthusiasm he would have applied to his learning. It doesn't matter what the job is; all that matters is that we are serving Hashem. We are like a White House assistant who is hired to do what the President needs us to do. The assistant doesn't tell the President, "I know you want me to work on that report, but I scheduled myself for several meetings today." He accepts the task the President gives him and does it to the best of his ability, because his only real job is to serve the President.

Serving Hashem while living in our complicated world demands flexibility. With so many people, situations, and needs swirling around us, we can only do our best to stay on track, all the while knowing that if Hashem switches the track, we're not being derailed. We're still on our way to the destination He has chosen for us. It's just a different route than we expected.

BASED ON A TRUE STORY

The man was lying in his bed, weak from illness. His family and doctors all insisted that he must eat, but he wouldn't. It was Yom Kippur. "I've never eaten on Yom Kippur and I'm not starting now," he said. "Hashem will take care of me."

However, the situation was dangerous. The family asked the Rabbi to speak to the patient and convince him that he was permitted to eat.

The Rabbi entered the patient's room and spoke to him. "You're not allowed to endanger your life by fasting," he explained. "It's no mitzvah to fast under these circumstances."

But the man would not be persuaded. "I'm not giving myself any excuses to eat," he said. "I can do it. I can fast."

"Alright," the Rabbi told him. "But if that's the case, I don't know if you'll be able to have an aliyah in shul anymore. We don't give an aliyah to someone who worships avodah zarah."

"What? What do you mean?" the man asked.

"If you're fasting when the halachah is that you should be eating, then you're worshiping the fast, not Hashem," he explained. "Right now, your avodah is to eat."

Hashem assigns us our "job" from day to day, from moment to moment. No matter what we think we should be doing, He shows us exactly what we're here to do.

MAKE IT REAL:

When your good intentions are derailed by circumstances, see what is needed and do it with the thought that, "This is what Hashem wants from me right now."

60

A Light at the End of the Tunnel

Never say never.

Azriel was dating. While most of his friends found their bashert quickly, he dated one girl after another. Something was always missing. Someone always broke off the shidduch. Azriel didn't feel as if he were any closer to getting married. Rather, he felt that he was permanently dating. After three years of dating, he met his wife. Suddenly, he was no longer dating. He was married. It happened just like that. Three years of dating seemed to fade quickly into history.

So often, when we are in a difficult situation, we feel as if it will never be over. We feel as if we'll be forever looking for a job, forever in-between yeshivos, forever sick, forever in limbo. However, there is a famous saying that tells us not to despair, but rather to watch for "the light at the end of the tunnel." Imagine walking through a tunnel that is so long that you can't see the light at the other end. You have no idea whether you'll be walking one mile, ten miles, or 50 miles till you find the exit. You don't know when you'll ever see the sun and breathe the fresh air again. You can imagine the trapped, miserable feeling of such an experience.

What would keep your spirits up? What would motivate you to keep going? Only the knowledge that there *is* an end to the tunnel. You would keep your eyes focused on the path ahead and watch hopefully for that first hint of light.

This is what Dovid HaMelech (*Tehillim* 130:7) advises when he tells us, "*Yachel Yisrael el Hashem ki im Hashem ha'chesed v'harbei Imo f'dus* — Let Yisrael hope for Hashem, for with Hashem is kindness and with Him is abundant redemption." In other words, He has millions of ways to take us out of our difficult situation and because of His infinite kindness, we can trust that He will help us. One moment we're walking in the dark and the next, we will see that glimmer of light. Although we won't see it until we arrive at the spot Hashem has chosen for our salvation, if we just keep reminding ourselves that it's there, we can keep going strong until we reach it.

As this book is being written, while the coronavirus is still turning our lives upside-down, this trust in the light at the end of the tunnel has become especially important. We want the world to go "back to normal" but the virus stubbornly keeps reappearing. We want to be able to pray together, learn together, celebrate each other's *simchos,* share Yamim Tovim with our families — to be together with all the warmth and closeness we enjoyed in the past, and without all the rules, restrictions, and fears.

In our desire to restore all these aspects of life that are so precious to us, we may put our trust in the wrong places. Public officials promise us that masks will keep us safe. Scientists promise that treatments are on the way. Politicians tell us that they have a plan to bring the virus under control. But with each new piece of expert advice and each new promise, we see more clearly than ever that we're not out of the tunnel yet, and no human being can make it shorter for us. Only Hashem knows where, when, and how we will see the light; we can trust Him to show it to us at exactly the right time.

One thought that can weaken our trust is, "What if we don't deserve Hashem's help?" This is like asking what if your two-year-old brother doesn't deserve his supper. *Can* he possibly deserve his supper? Of course not. Your mother feeds him because she loves him and wants to care for him. She knows he is only a baby; he will cry, get into mischief, spill things and break things. Likewise, Hashem knows that we are only human. We will make mistakes, we will commit sins, we will try to improve and then slide back again. That is why Dovid HaMelech (*Tehillim* 130:8) reassures us that "He [Hashem] will redeem Yisrael from its sins." More than we need to be saved from our troubles, we need to be saved from the sins that bring us our troubles. Hashem, Who created us, knows us, and loves us, will do this for us as long as we do *teshuvah* and try to improve ourselves. We just have to keep moving through the tunnel, knowing He is guiding us to the light at the end.

MAKE IT REAL:

If you feel stuck in a difficult situation, remind yourself that one small change can change everything. There is always a light at the end of the tunnel.

61

Let's Be Honest

You'll never get lost if you just go straight.

It only takes a second for our minds to figure out a reason for just a little cheating. Perhaps some of these phrases are familiar to you:

- No one will ever know.
- It won't hurt anyone.
- I'll just borrow it and give it right back.
- Everyone does it.
- I don't have to try to be a *tzaddik*.
- They're not serious about this rule.

We often think that the "smart" person cuts corners, reads between the lines, and understands that "rules are made to be broken," while the foolish person puts himself at a disadvantage by naively doing as he's told. For example, the student who gets his older brother to write his essay for him gets an A while the student who persists on doing his own work gets a B.

In the short run, this assessment might be correct. People seem to make money through clever but not-quite-honest business schemes. They seem to get jobs and advantages by buying their way into a situation that is better than what they would deserve on their own merit. However, a person with *bitachon* is not fooled by these false pictures. *Tehillim* (24:3-4) tells us that if we want to "climb to the top of Hashem's mountain" and "stand in a holy place," the requirement is "clean hands." What are clean hands? They are hands that have not touched what does not belong to them.

Dovid HaMelech is describing a righteous person who, because of his honesty, will earn great spiritual rewards. However, we are living in the here and now, in the physical world. It can be difficult to take the high road when the reward for doing so seems very far away, and the benefit of a little dishonesty seems very close at hand. Therefore, we need to realize that even in this world, the honest person often achieves success.

Yaakov Avinu was a prime example. Lavan tried to cheat him many times, but Yaakov remained honest. He replaced all of Lavan's animals that were lost or injured and took such good care of Lavan's flocks that all of their offspring were born alive and healthy. Despite all Lavan had done to Yaakov, Yaakov never thought that he had a right to take advantage of his position of trust. He patiently and loyally served Lavan until the time came for him to leave. In the end, Yaakov became incredibly wealthy.

We may not see it immediately, but honesty always pays. One of its greatest rewards is the positive image we have of ourselves and that others have of us when we are people who can be trusted.

A True Story

Daniel had leased a car, and he had been tough on it. He drove it 11,000 miles past the limit that the lease contract allowed. Also, the car had many bumps and scratches for which he was responsible. He dreaded the day that he had to give it back to the lease company because he knew it would cost him plenty of money, money that he didn't have.

"You know," his coworker told him, "there's a way to turn back the odometer to make the mileage look lower. They'll never know. This way at least you won't have to pay for all those extra miles."

"That's dishonest," Daniel answered. "And it won't do any good, because Hashem is in charge of money. Whatever amount I save will just go out some other way."

Daniel returned the car. "Someone will look it over and

get back to you with the amount you owe," the agent told him.

A week later, Daniel hadn't heard from the lease company. He called for an update.

"You owed $4,000," the agent told him, "but not anymore. Someone wanted to buy the car and he had to get rid of the debt first, so he paid up what you owed."

To Daniel, this was Hashem's voice telling him loud and clear that he had done the right thing. He didn't have to resort to dishonesty. If Hashem wanted him to be spared the expense, He had many ways of fulfilling His plan. But even if the reward hadn't been so obviously connected to Daniel's choice, it would still have been the right choice. Honesty is the road to self-respect, a good reputation, and greatness.

MAKE IT REAL:

Listen to your thoughts when you're making a decision and be alert to the suggestions like those listed above that can lead you to dishonesty.

62

The Gift You'd Never Ask For

Embarrassment can be beautiful.

Among the things we pray for in our morning blessings is to be saved from *bushah,* embarrassment. Few feelings are as miserable. When a person is embarrassed, his face flushes, his stomach flip-flops, and he truly wishes he could "fall through the floor," out of the view of anyone who has witnessed his humiliation. Embarrassing another person is even compared to killing him.

It might be surprising then to learn that Rav Bension Kripes once saw the Chofetz Chaim crying bitter tears over the fact that he was never shamed. On the contrary, wherever he went, people treated him with great honor. What was the problem with that? "Chazal teach us that there is no atonement in the world like that of being shamed," he told Rabbi Kripes. The Chofetz Chaim bemoaned the fact that he would never have this atonement, and he would have to go on to the Next World and face judgment without this benefit.

This is hard for us to understand because most people would do anything to avoid being embarrassed. Also, if shame is such a gift, why do we pray for Hashem to save us from it? The reason for that prayer is that being embarrassed is a difficult test, which the average person must try to avoid for fear of failure. However, if it happens anyway, we might as well reap the benefits that are just sitting there, waiting for us to grab. We might as well realize that Hashem is handing us an opportunity to become pure and clean of any sins we might have committed.

To gain this benefit, a person has to resist the urge to hate or seek revenge against the person who has embarrassed him. Instead, he has to accept that nothing happens unless Hashem wills it; the messenger is only a messenger. This is the way Dovid HaMelech responded when Shimi ben Geira cursed him. Dovid's companions offered to kill Shimi for his disrespect to the king, but Dovid said, "Let him be; let him curse, for Hashem has told him to."

When we manage to accept embarrassment in this spirit, the humble heart we display erases our own sins. We show Hashem that we accept His will and we don't consider our own pride to be the most important thing. This is a powerful form of *teshuvah*.

In our everyday life, if we have happy, healthy friendships and family relationships, we might be fortunate enough to encounter embarrassing situations very rarely. However, a person doesn't have to be cursed like Dovid HaMelech or thrown out of a party like Bar Kamtza to be embarrassed. How do you feel when you give a wrong answer in class? When you make an error that costs your team points, or perhaps the whole game? When your classmates are yawning as you give your oral report? When you forget an important chore your parents asked you to do? When you have to tell your friends that you failed your driving test?

Knowing that *bushah* does so much for us, you can turn any of these circumstances into a golden opportunity for *teshuvah*. Think to yourself, "I'm just going to face what happened and accept people's reactions. I'm not going to do the same thing back to them. I'm not going to be angry." So much good can result.

A True Story

In a neighborhood in Yerushalayim, a young woman named Tzipporah came to the local grocery store to help her mother bring home their packages. Accidentally, she took several bags that were sitting on the counter that belonged to the store's cashier. Later, the cashier saw that her bags were missing and checked* *the security camera. On the video, she saw Tzipporah taking her bags.*

The next time Tzipporah's mother came in, the cashier saw her and screamed at her that her daughter was a thief. She showed her a snapshot from the video to prove her point. The mother explained that there had been a mistake, which they had realized when they unpacked the groceries. Since the store was closed by that hour, they brought the items back the next day. The cashier was not quite appeased. Worse yet, Tzipporah was in shidduchim, and this accusation, screamed in the middle of the neighborhood grocery store, could only do harm.

When the mother arrived home, she told her daughter the story. "What's going to be with a shidduch for you after something like this?" the mother said. She wanted to take the cashier to beis din for slandering them. Tzipporah, however, had a different idea. It was 11 Cheshvan, Rachel Imeinu's yahrtzeit. Rachel, who had saved her older sister Leah from humiliation by allowing Yaakov to marry her, was the one Tzipporah wanted to emulate. She decided to go to the store and straighten things out. To seal the peace, she bought the cashier a box of chocolates. And Tzipporah found her shidduch, just as she knew she would.

MAKE IT REAL:

The next time you feel that flush of embarrassment rising to your face, turn on your emunah and turn the test into a berachah.

63

Look How Far You've Come!

When you look back, you see that you're getting somewhere.

You decide to improve your physical strength, so you buy some 20-pound weights and begin working out. Your friend, who has been working out for a year already, lifts 50-pound weights. Would you expect, after a few weeks of working out, to be able to lift 50 pounds as well? If that were your expectation, you'd probably abandon your work-out quickly, thinking, "This isn't getting me anywhere!" Most people understand that even though they haven't reached their goal, they are getting stronger every day.

However, when we make a resolution to improve our *middos* or *avodas Hashem,* we often expect instant results. For example, it's Elul and you say to yourself, "I'm done being a hot-head. Anger is like *avodah zarah*! From now on, whatever happens, I'm going to keep my cool." Before Rosh Hashanah has even arrived, you're despairing that your temper hasn't gone away. Or perhaps you decide that you will say your *berachos* with more concentration. You even manage to do it for a day or two, but you soon morph back into your old mumble-jumble. These false starts make us feel that we really can't change; we give up trying.

The secret to spiritual growth, and certainly to becoming a *baal emunah,* is to realize that it's not a project we can start and finish; it's a path we choose to follow for a lifetime.

There will always be people who are far ahead of us on the path. Maybe they started out ahead because of their nature or their upbringing, or maybe they've just been working on their *emunah* for a longer time. However, no one who reads all about *emunah,* "learns how to do it" and "gets it done" immediately.

Therefore, if you're trying to put more *emunah* into your life but you find yourself reacting to situations in the same old way, this is not a signal that you haven't changed. The more you keep going back to your learning and focus on *emunah,* the more it will become a part of you. As new situations arise, you'll find that you really do handle them differently than you would have before you set your goal of building *emunah.*

We should not focus on how far we need to go. We should not think about the great *baalei emunah* in *Klal Yisrael* and compare ourselves unfavorably to them. Instead, we should think about ourselves and look for situations that show our progress. "That would have gotten me furious when I was younger," you might realize. Or perhaps there are issues that you used to find frightening or worrisome, and now you are able to say, "Hashem will take care of it." Look how far you've gotten and you won't give up the effort. You'll see that, like the weight-lifter, you've been able to add a pound or two at a time. You can't lift the 50-pound weights yet, but you've moved well past the 20-pounders.

Is it worth the effort? It is when you look at people who have been "at it" all their lives. Their level of happiness, calm, and contentment is worth every day of the effort it takes to get there.

- *One day, someone said something extremely disrespectful to Rav Yechezkel Levenstein. A few minutes later, a student saw that he wore a big smile. "Rebbi, how could you be so happy after that?" his student asked. "Baruch Hashem, I didn't open my mouth to respond to the person who attacked me," he answered. "Hashem helped me to believe completely that this was from Him. I'm so excited by what I accomplished!"*
- *Rav Elchanan Wasserman needed to raise money for his yeshivah. He asked an important member of his community*

to come with him, but the man was apprehensive about being rejected or embarrassed by asking for donations. Rav Wasserman told him, "If Heaven has decreed that a person will experience shame, he can't escape it. But it can come to him in many different ways. The fortunate person gets his share of shame while doing something for the sake of Hashem."

- And what about ordinary people? *A Rabbi was walking along a city street with a man he knew to have strong emunah. A car drove through a puddle and splashed the man's clothing, but he just kept walking as if nothing happened. A security guard outside the next building said, "What a calm reaction. I would have gone crazy!" Hearing the comment, the man told the Rabbi, "It was from Hashem. Why be upset?"*

We need to hear these stories to see what lies ahead if we stay on the road. Just as important, however, is to look behind us, see where we were and, like Rav Yechezkel, celebrate how far we've come.

MAKE IT REAL:

Think of one situation you've put into better perspective since you began working on your emunah.

64

Pitiful or Powerful? We Choose

Our hardships don't define us.

A classmate seems to have one purpose for coming to school — to disrupt the class. Her outbursts often get a laugh, but really, everyone is embarrassed for her. She makes a fool of herself. People are polite enough to her, but no one considers her a friend. Well-meaning teachers who try to make a connection to her never get very far. Only a few people know that behind this girl's unruly behavior is a family that lives in chaos. The parents argue with each other and scream at the children. Her overwhelmed mother prepares dinner only when she's in the mood, which is not often. The father is fired from job after job. Your classmate, the oldest child, basically runs the household.

When we hear a story like this, we think, "Well, what could we expect from this poor girl!" If she were to leave the path of Torah, drop out of school, or become involved in risky behaviors, we would not be surprised. After all, she's suffered so much.

In fact, we should have compassion and understanding for this girl who must face difficult challenges. We can never know how we would survive in such a situation and certainly can't judge another person's reaction. However, for the girl herself, "What can anyone expect from me?" is a counterproductive idea. It turns her into a victim whose life will always be darkened by her challenging circumstances. Indeed, even if she has a difficult childhood, by clinging to this picture of herself as a victim, she will have a difficult adulthood as well.

At a certain point, we all have to look at our lives, our upbringing, the unfairness and challenges we may have faced, and say, "OK, that's what happened in the past. I have to accept that it was from Hashem, deal with it, and make something of myself." Surely Hashem's purpose for us cannot be to simply drift around in a pool of grievances forever. We're each meant to get somewhere and we're given the tools to do it. Sometimes, the terrible situation is actually a powerful tool; it may show us what our mission is and motivate us to achieve it.

Our first step is to realize that Hashem places each child in the family that is right for him and gives each set of parents the children who are right for them. Even if a family seems to the child to be a terrible fit, it is that exact challenge that Hashem has put into his life to help form him into the person he needs to be. (**Please note that even if we accept our situation, we must still seek help in improving and dealing with it**.) Hashem knows exactly what we need to experience. Our job is to grow from the experience.

When Rabbi Yaakov Yosef Herman (1880-1967) was 13, his parents placed him with cousins in America while they returned to Europe. As part of the agreement, Rabbi Herman had to pay the family $1 a week in rent. One Friday afternoon, the cousins told him that they were raising his rent to $1.25. Since he could not pay the higher amount, they threw him out. Sobbing and shocked at their cruelty, he ran from the house. He spent that Shabbos night sleeping on a park bench. When he awoke, he promised himself that when he married and had his own home, he would never sit down for a Shabbos or Yom Tov meal without guests around his table.

He held on to his goal and became renowned for his hospitality. People from all walks of life, from great Rabbanim to troubled souls, found their way to his table. For many years, there was no such thing as having "nowhere to go for Shabbos," because the Hermans' door was always open.

Imagine being a poor teenager alone in America, being kicked out of your home and left to fend for yourself on the streets of New York. If Rabbi Herman had turned against Hashem at this point, who could have blamed him? But he didn't question Hashem. Instead, he took stock of the situation, learned from it, and found power in it. He would be the one to make sure this didn't happen to anyone else. He would make sure that every Jew within his reach, even those who wandered the streets all week, would have a seat at the Shabbos table.

When we accept that our situation is just as Hashem has planned and is *necessary* for us to discover and accomplish our mission in life, we become powerful rather than pitiful. Being a victim might feel good for a while, but being productive, accomplished, and grateful to Hashem feels good forever.

MAKE IT REAL:

Do you feel that you are a victim in some way? If so, ask yourself what Hashem might want you to gain from this situation and think of at least one way you can make something positive of it.

65

Who Owes Whom?

Mitzvos are a gift to you!

A 14-year-old boy has a challenge. He just can't get himself to bed at a reasonable hour. Because of that, he can't get himself out of bed in the morning. He often misses *minyan* and has to "speed-*daven*" at home in order to get to yeshivah on time. This boy has another challenge as well: His cousin, to whom he is very close, is in the hospital, sick with a life-threatening disease. The boy decides to make a "deal" with Hashem. He will get to *minyan* every morning and in return, Hashem will heal his cousin. When his cousin's condition gets worse instead of better, what is this boy's reaction?

If he is like many people, he will think, "Hashem, I've worked so hard to do this mitzvah for you. Why haven't you done what I asked in return?" In other words, they feel that because they have put in extra effort to serve Hashem, Hashem owes them a reward.

We often try to put more energy into our *avodas Hashem* when we want something from Him, hoping that we'll be able to earn merit that will help us. This is a normal and useful approach to a difficult situation, and we hear many stories of miracles that have occurred this way.

Where we go wrong is in seeing this as a deal: "I'll do this for You, Hashem, and in return, You'll do that for me." When we view our mitzvos as "our end of the deal," but Hashem — in His far greater understanding of what our soul needs — does not keep up His end, we see our mitzvah as wasted. It's as if we paid for something on Amazon and the package never came.

This point of view is truly upside-down and backwards. If we think we are doing anything at all for Hashem when we do a mitzvah, we are blind to what is really happening. The reality is more like this:

> *Parents notice their daughter is a talented artist. They pay hundreds of dollars to give her art lessons and buy her an easel and a supply of expensive paints and canvases. They encourage her by asking her to paint a picture for a specific spot on the living room wall. The daughter spends weeks painting a beautiful picture for her parents. They admire it and hang it in its perfect spot. Later that day, the daughter says, "Ma, remember I asked you yesterday if I could buy those new shoes I saw? Can I buy them today?" "I'm sorry, but I think it's not a good idea. You have so many shoes. Let's wait until Pesach to buy more." The daughter is angry: "After I just gave her this painting I spent weeks on, she won't even buy me a pair of shoes," she thinks.*

The daughter's complaint is ridiculous; the only reason she is able to paint a beautiful picture at all is because her parents have given her everything she needed to do it, starting with life itself. The only reason they asked her to paint something for them was to make her feel valued. She thinks she's giving them a gift, but the real gift is the opportunity her parents gave her to develop her talent. Instead of feeling that they owe her something, she should feel grateful: "Thank you, Daddy and Mommy, for giving me art lessons so I could make this painting!"

Likewise, when we do a mitzvah, we are simply using the gifts Hashem has given us to do something for Him — something He does not need. Nevertheless, He gives us mitzvos to do so that we can feel the pleasure of serving Him, doing something in return for the countless gifts He gives us. On top of that, He rewards us in the Next World for our efforts. It is a deal, but it's a one-way deal: We only gain and Hashem only gives.

He gives us the intelligence to learn Torah, as well as the freedom (think of the *Yevanim* and the Soviet Union) to attend Jewish schools. He gives us families to feed and care for us so that we are physically able to learn, pray, and do mitzvos. Our vision, our hearing, our friends and teachers — they are all opportunities Hashem gives us. Why? Just so we can enjoy the pleasure of serving Him and feeling close to Him in this world, and the great, indescribable pleasure of our reward in the World to Come.

MAKE IT REAL:

When you undertake a mitzvah as a merit for something you want, make sure to tell yourself that the mitzvah is its own reward, and if Hashem answers your request, that is "icing on the cake."

66

Even Hashem is impressed by our emunah.

Imagine being Avraham Avinu. Every single person in the world worships idols, but you believe in Hashem. How would you stick to your beliefs? How could you be strong enough to know with certainty that you are right and the rest of the world is wrong? How would you have the courage and confidence to try to teach other people about Hashem? Living in a society filled with false beliefs makes true beliefs difficult or impossible to hold on to.

Even so, all our *Avos* lived with great *emunah* while the world around them lived in darkness. Because of Yitzchak's *emunah,* he was willing to be offered as a sacrifice. Because of Yaakov's *emunah,* he was able to remain faithful while living with the crooked Lavan, having Dina abducted by Shechem, being pursued by his brother Esav, and not knowing what happened to his beloved son Yosef for 22 years. In fact, because of all he endured, he became the greatest *baal emunah* of all the *Avos.*

This unquestioning trust in Hashem even in the darkest times is what makes the *Avos* so beloved by Hashem. "I miss the *Avos* so much," He told Moshe Rabbeinu. "There was no one like them. There were so many times they could have questioned Me, but they never did" (*Shemos Rabbah* 6:4).

If we look at the world around us now, we see that it is once again becoming dark. Fifty years ago, most people believed in G-d in some way, according to their religion. Today, even "educated" people think G-d is a superstition, and the morals our world has lived by for centuries, all based in Torah, are old-fashioned. These anti-religious ideas have been taught in public schools and colleges for so long that they've seeped into every corner of our society. People are so confused that when an actual *mageifah* — the world-wide plague of Covid-19 — comes down from Heaven, they can't hear Hashem's voice shouting, "This is from Me! I want you to do *teshuvah*!" Instead, they look to scientists and politicians to take the blame and find the cure.

In our personal lives, as well, people experience many kinds of darkness. They struggle for *parnassah,* can't find their *zivug,* or struggle with Torah and learning. Some parents worry that their children are heading off the path of Torah. We see long lists of names of people who need a *refuah sheleimah.*

This would all be very frightening if it were not exactly as the *Midrash* says life will be in the days before Mashiach: Hashem's Presence will be hidden and we will live in darkness as the *Avos* did. Many things will happen that make no sense.

Why would Hashem allow the world to reach this state? It is to give us the chance to attain the highest heights of *emunah.* A light shines brightest when it is surrounded by darkness. If we were surrounded by good, wholesome people in a wholesome culture, remaining true to the Torah would not require much effort. However, we are now living in an unwholesome, unbelieving world. We are in the position of Avraham Avinu, who stood on one side while the rest of the world stood on the other. We now have the opportunity, through our *emunah,* to arouse Hashem's greatest outpouring of love. The *navi* Zechariah (8:6) tells us that Hashem is actually amazed by our *emunah* in difficult times: "Just as it will be wondrous in the eyes of the remnant of this people in those days, so will it be wondrous in My eyes."

> *It's more than 3,300 years since the Jewish people received the holy Torah from Hashem. For nearly 2,000 of those years, we've been in exile, living among other cultures and religions. How is it even possible that we are still keeping Shabbos, still separating milk from meat, eating*

only the animals and fish the Torah permits, banning chametz for the week of Pesach, building little huts in our yards on Succos, dipping our dishes in a mikvah? How is it possible that we still look toward Hashem, Who hasn't revealed Himself to us since the year 2448 at Har Sinai, to help us in our times of need, or that we recognize His hand in nature? How have we held on so tightly for so long?

With every *tefillah,* every mitzvah, every *"Im yirtzeh Hashem"* and *"Gam zu l'tovah"* we sincerely say, we become more and more amazing in Hashem's eyes. May He soon break through the darkness and light up the world with the coming of Mashiach!

MAKE IT REAL:

Use the next opportunity when you see Jews performing a mitzvah together — menorahs on Chanukah or biur chametz or succah building or just heading to shul for Shabbos davening — to say to yourself, "After thousands of years, we're still doing it!"

67

Do Yourself the Biggest Favor

When we forgive others, Hashem forgives us

When someone wrongs us, they are delivering to our doorstep a large cardboard box filled with *nisyonos*. What do we find when we open it? We find many tests of our *middos*: Will we react with anger? Will we say something cruel and hurtful to the person? Will we speak *lashon hara* about him? Will we try to get back at him, and in doing so, violate the Torah's law against seeking revenge? Will we hold a grudge, promising ourselves that we'll never forgive him?

These appear to be many different tests, but they all have the same answer: *emunah*. When we calm down, think about what happened, and realize that it could have happened only if it was what Hashem wanted, then all the other tests disappear. Why be angry at the person who was only delivering Hashem's message? Why bring *aveiros* on ourselves by speaking hurtfully or spreading *lashon hara* or seeking revenge or holding a grudge? None of these reactions make sense anymore when we view the situation through *emunah* lenses.

"Yes, but that lets the other person off the hook!" a person might think. "He did something wrong. Why should he get away with it?"

In a way, this thought is correct. If we can find a peaceful way to right a wrong, we should do so. A parent, teacher, rebbi, or Rav might be able to help straighten out the situation. Once we've done that, however, we still might not be happy with the outcome or with the person with whom we are in conflict. So now what? Do we go through life with a sore spot in our heart? Do we have to feel a wave of dislike whenever we run into the person or hear his name mentioned?

If we strengthen our *emunah,* we can be free of our negative feelings. We can forgive, and when we do, we gain everything and lose nothing. The first benefit a person notices when he forgives is that he feels so much better! It's as if he's been moping around in a gloomy room and all of a sudden, he thinks, "Hey, why don't I turn on the light!" The moment he flicks the switch, he feels happier and more energetic.

The most astounding benefit, however, is the one we receive from Hashem. The Gemara (*Rosh Hashanah* 17a) states that "Whoever forgives and overlooks a wrong done to him is forgiven for all his sins." Read those words again — *all his sins*! How could that even be? It happens because forgiving a wrong demands extraordinary strength, *mesirus nefesh,* and *emunah.* We know that "according to the difficulty is the reward," and that is why the reward for forgiveness is so great. For this reason, forgiving others is a powerful *segulah* when we need Hashem's help.

It is far from easy to be the one to make the first move, to break the ice and reach out to an adversary with an offer for peace. However, as a woman who mediates complicated, long-term family feuds once reported, "No one is ever unhappy that he did it." A true story (names are changed) from Rav Lugassi helps us see the power of forgiveness in action:

A True Story

When Rachel was in high school in Eretz Yisrael, she had a wealthy classmate who looked down on her and her poor family. The girl's comments and attitude ruined Rachel's self-esteem. This stood in the way of her finding a shidduch, and at 28, she was still alone. One day, Rachel ran into another high-school friend, Leba. When Leba asked how Rachel was doing, Rachel confided in her that she was unhappy and was still suffering from the rich girl's demeaning attitude.

Leba decided to try to find the classmate and make peace. She reached the woman in the United States, where she had settled, and found out that although her life was good, she had been married for years and had not been able to have children. Leba told her about the pain she had caused Rachel and suggested that making peace with her would be a great segulah for having a child. The woman was shocked to find out that her childish cruelty had such long-lasting effects. She decided to fly to Eretz Yisrael to seek forgiveness in person.

Rachel wasn't able to forgive easily; the pain was deep. The two women met a few times until Rachel felt she could sincerely overcome her grievance and forgive her classmate with a whole heart. As they hugged each other good-bye, the woman predicted that Rachel would soon be married, and promised to come to her wedding. In fact, Rachel was married that year, but the friend didn't keep her promise. She was in labor with her first child!

MAKE IT REAL:

Are you holding a grudge against anyone? Think of the rewards of letting it go and take the first step toward making peace.

68

Expect Miracles

Hashem is greater than your greatest challenge.

"It's no use. It's impossible. There's no way this is going to get better. The odds are against us. We can't possibly win."

These are the words of a person who can only see through one eye — the *Olam Hazeh* eye. That is the eye that sees the material world in front of us and understands the rules that control that world. To this person, everything operates according to logic, science, and nature. When troubles come up, there's no hope unless it rests on proof he can see and understand.

For the Jewish people, however, this view of the world is false. The Gemara (*Shabbos* 31a) tells us that one of the questions we will be asked when we arrive in *Shamayim* at the end of our life is, "Did you eagerly await the *yeshuah*?" This is usually interpreted to mean that we are required to await Mashiach's arrival. The *Beis HaLevi* (*Mitzvos HaBitachon*) gives us another meaning, which is that we will be asked if we awaited Hashem's *yeshuah* for our troubles, no matter how bleak the situation.

The key word here is "await." When we await something, we are expecting it to arrive. We're not just passing the time as we do when we're sitting in the dentist's waiting room. "Awaiting" means that we must eagerly expect our *yeshuah*. We don't know how or when, but we are certain that it will come. Unlike just passively waiting, eagerly awaiting an event changes how we feel and what we do. When a person awaits a bus that he knows will arrive, he stands at the bus stop glancing down the road, his luggage ready by his side. If the bus is taking him some place he really wants to go, he feels excitement as he waits.

When we see beyond the rules of logic, science, and nature, we know that no matter how unlikely our *yeshuah* seems in a practical sense, we can confidently await it. As Moshe told the Jewish people when the Egyptians pursued them to the *Yam Suf*, "Stand fast and see the salvation of Hashem that He will perform for you today" (*Shemos* 14:13). Hashem created the system of nature and He can "split the Sea" for us any time He wishes.

With *emunah,* we live under a different system than does the rest of the world. We are Hashem's treasured nation, and He tends to each of us directly, lovingly. We must always expect His salvation, no matter what the experts and statistics tell us. This alone can lift us up out of a difficult situation.

> *Years ago, the 14-year-old son of Rabbi Yisrael Brog was diagnosed with multiple sclerosis, an incurable disease that attacks a person's nervous system. The doctor told the father and son about the many health challenges they could expect in the future. When they got in their car to return home, Rabbi Brog's son asked him, "Does this mean I'm going to die young?"*
>
> *Rabbi Brog answered, "I've been working on my emunah and bitachon my entire life. We've seen with our own eyes so many miracles. We are going to get through this calmly. When there's a health problem that has a regular cure, we have to do as much hishtadlus as we can, but if no one knows of a cure, we can confidently rely only on Hashem, the Rofei cholei amo Yisrael. He has a cure for this and b'ezras Hashem, He'll show it to us."*
>
> *As they visited various doctors who specialized in the disease, Rabbi Brog reminded his son not to pay attention to their warnings about what the future would hold. He told one doctor, "In medical school, they taught*

you that there is no cure for this disease and according to the book, you are right. But I have a G-d Who doesn't go by the book, and I could tell you stories that I have witnessed to prove it."

In fact, the doctors' dire predictions did not come about. The son's condition remained mild. He was even able to marry and have children. While the doctors waited for disaster, the Brogs awaited their yeshuah.

MAKE IT REAL:

Do you have a challenge that seems unlikely to resolve? Change your outlook by reminding yourself that no matter what obstacles you see, Hashem can remove them in a second.

69

Your Honor

There's never enough recognition to feel satisfied.

Imagine a person who doesn't have enough to eat. He goes to bed hungry every night. Keeping his *emunah* strong is not easy; after all, his grumbling stomach continually reminds him that his needs are not being taken care of — at least not at that moment. Now imagine a person who has a packed refrigerator and overflowing pantry, but is missing the one food he really craves. Therefore, he refuses to eat anything else and he goes to bed hungry, just like the poor man.

Clearly, the second man has created his own problem. He's turned away from all the good he's been given and chosen to chase after something that is out of reach. He feels deprived when he should feel perfectly satisfied.

This is the life of a person who chases after other people's approval and admiration. He wants it, needs it, believes he deserves it, and won't be content until he gets it. Even if his life is packed with everything else he needs to succeed, every time other people fail to recognize his "greatness," he is insulted and unhappy. Everything he does is aimed at attracting recognition. His life is filled with non-stop stress.

If sometimes you look around for honor and recognition, keep in mind that "Wealth and honor come from You [Hashem]" (*I Divrei HaYamim* 29:12). Just as a person of *emunah* realizes that no one can deprive him of money Hashem has assigned to him, he knows that no one can deprive him of honor, either.

Will people notice how smart you are? How much *tzedakah* you raised? What a big favor you've done? And if they don't, will you feel deprived? Will you "go to bed hungry" even though you have everything you need? Hashem sends honor our way only when it will do good — when it will encourage us to keep striving or perhaps inspire others to follow our lead.

This true story (with names changed) teaches us that honor is a "dangerous substance" that only Hashem can measure correctly:

> *Rabbi Schwartz* was a young man, but he had already developed a powerful speaking style that pierced his listeners' hearts. Gradually, his talents became known and a major Jewish organization contracted with him to produce recorded shiurim that would be distributed throughout the English-speaking world.*
>
> *This was in the days when tape cassettes were the most up-to-date recording method, and Rabbi Schwartz's lecture series was going to be sold as a set in a tape binder. On the back of the binder would normally be a few lines identifying the speaker and praising his speaking style. The writer who prepared those lines wanted to convey the unusual ability with words this speaker possessed. However, when the speaker saw what had been written, he was uncomfortable. He showed them to his Rav, who told him, "Don't even put your name on the outside of the binder."*
>
> *To the writer, it seemed inconceivable that such a talented speaker would not be named and acknowledged. To the speaker, however, it was not an issue at all. His Rav had advised him not to become a "star" at a young age. Perhaps the praise would go to his head, even a little, and dampen the fire of his speeches. He knew that no one was denying him honor. It simply wasn't his to possess at that time.*

If you teach yourself not to be hungry for honor, you'll go through life feeling calm and satisfied. You'll realize that no one can take away what wasn't meant for you in the first place.

MAKE IT REAL:

Try doing a "secret kindness" for someone — an anonymous favor that you do without seeking recognition. Or, if you are often called on in class, try holding back on answering a question to allow someone else to answer.

70

"I Never Get Tired of You"

Hashem's love is there for us at all times.

Imagine a little boy who idolizes his big brother. The brother loves the cute little boy as well. He is happy to give him shoulder rides and read him stories and listen to his mixed-up tales of playgroup adventures. But after a while, the big brother says, "OK, no more for now. I have things I need to do."

That's human love. Even if it's always there beneath the surface, we can't always express it. We run out of time, strength, or patience. An adult child might tend to a sick parent with great care and tenderness, but eventually, the child must go take care of his own family or his own needs. In another example, a mother might gladly take care of her child when the child is young and can't do much for himself, but as the child grows older, the mother pulls back. "You're old enough to take care of that yourself," she might say.

How different from this is Hashem's love! His greatest desire is that we attach ourselves to Him and never let go. "And to Him you should cleave," says the Torah (*Devarim* 10:20). The word "cleave" means to stick to something perfectly, like wallpaper to a wall. If we prayed to Him 100 times a day, He would treasure our 100th prayer as much as our first. In fact, He would be even more pleased and delighted by the 101st prayer. We cannot imagine any human being, no matter how much he loved us, being delighted with our 101st request of the day.

This fact — that Hashem is always available to us and *wants* us to depend on Him — gives us the most important piece of information we can have for living a happy life. Hashem loves us. Hashem loves YOU. Every minute of every day is a time when He is available. You need only think of Him, feel His Presence all around you, and speak to Him. Share your worries with Him and ask Him to help you. Ask Him for strength to go through whatever challenges lie ahead. Ask Him to hold you and not let you go. He will never become tired of carrying you.

Feeling loved is a precious asset. Money cannot buy it and yet it does more for us than anything money can buy. Even scientific studies have proven the power of love. People who feel loved suffer less from depression. Their blood pressure is lower. They worry less, even when they face tough challenges. They heal faster after an illness or an accident. They feel less pain. They even catch fewer colds. All these benefits are ours because we are the beloved children of Hashem. A Jew should never feel, "Nobody loves me."

But to gain the benefits of Hashem's constant love, we have to notice it. The more we focus on all that He gives us — the big gifts and the small ones — the more we will feel loved, and the more we feel loved, the more strength, confidence, and optimism we will have in our lives.

> *Learning in Eretz Yisrael had been Ari's dream for many years. But it was also his nightmare, because he was a quiet, introverted type of person and he worried that he would be lonely so far from home.*
>
> *When he was 20, he felt he was no longer progressing in the beis medrash where he had been learning since high school. After discussing the situation with his rebbi, he decided that he would take the leap and enroll in the Mir in Yerushalayim. His closest friends were staying put, and so he would be setting out alone on this new adventure.*
>
> *As the time approached for his departure, his heart and his mind seemed to be operating in two separate worlds. His mind was excited about the challenge and eager to experience life in Eretz Yisrael. His heart, however,*

was quietly pumping out fear and stress that upset his stomach and kept him wide awake at night.

At last, the day came. He found himself at the departure gate waiting to board his flight. Knowing that he would probably be filled with stress, he had taken along a Tehillim to steady his nerves. He let it flop open to a random page, where he found these words: "...Because he cleaves to Me, I will save him. I will strengthen him because he knows My Name. When he calls on Me, I will answer Him. I am with him in his troubles..." (91:14-15). Ari's fears began to fade and at last, he fully looked forward to what lay ahead. "I'm not in this alone," he told himself.

He turned to that chapter of Tehillim often during his first few months at the Mir. It carried him through every time.

MAKE IT REAL:

When something good happens or even when nothing particularly good happens, but you stop to see the good in your everyday life, remind yourself that you're experiencing Hashem's love. When you face a challenge, remember His love and ask Hashem to carry you through the situation.

71

The World Is Made for Giving

Hashem loves the poor and the rich...

If your father gives one of your siblings an allowance of $100 a week and another sibling $5 a week, the one who is getting the lesser amount would seem justified in thinking that "Daddy loves him more than me." People tend to think the same of Hashem; if He gives one person more money, better looks, a quicker mind or a greater talent, they think this is a sign that He loves that person more than those to whom He gives fewer material benefits.

We might be disturbed to discover that by holding that view, we are making the same mistake as the evil Roman general, Turnus Rufus, who asked Rabbi Akiva (*Bava Basra* 10a), "If G-d loves the poor so much, why doesn't He give them more money?" Rabbi Akiva answered, "Hashem loves the poor and the rich and He enables both to amass the merits they need to earn *Olam Haba*."

Rabbi Akiva is teaching us that Hashem knows what each soul needs. For the rich, the test is to use their money wisely. Will they give to those in need or will they try to hold on to every dollar for themselves? Will their wealth make them feel superior to others, or will they understand that it is only a gift Hashem has put into their hands for now? Will their business concerns take over their lives or will they learn Torah and *daven* as they should?

The tests of those in need might be easier to grasp: Will they be bitter about their situation? Will they be jealous of others who have more? Will they trust Hashem to give them what they need when they need it? Some souls require the tests of the wealthy while others can only earn their *Olam Haba* with the tests of the needy.

This balance of rich and poor not only helps individuals acquire merit, but also helps to elevate the entire Jewish people. In fact, it helps to hold up the world; as *Pirkei Avos* (1:2) states, "The world stands on three things: Torah, service to Hashem, and acts of kindness." Starting with our forefather Avraham, a love of *chesed* has been one of the Jewish "genetic traits" passed down through the generations. Jews have a natural love of helping each other, which we can easily see by the number of volunteer organizations we have to take care of every need. The Jewish people have groups like Hatzolah, whose volunteers run to medical emergencies any time of the day or night, sometimes risking their own lives. We have organizations that give people money for expensive medical treatments; that give pots, dishes, and linens to newlyweds; that change people's tires and unlock their cars; that loan out everything from lawnmowers to car seats to tablecloths for a *simchah*.

The basis of all these organizations and acts of kindness is that some people have a need and others have the ability to fill it. The result of all this giving and taking is a powerful, constantly flowing river of merit for the Jewish people. It's important to note that every person has times when he is the giver and other times when he is the taker. No one has it all, and no one has nothing to offer. By creating a world that depends on *chesed*, Hashem has given us the ultimate gift.

A true story from Rabbi Yoel Gold:

> *In 2011, Rabbi Yotav Eliach took 50 American high-school students on a tour of Israel. Before they returned home, they visited a cemetery where fallen Israeli soldiers were buried. The Rabbi movingly described the sacrifice of the families who sent their sons off to protect the Land.*
>
> *As he spoke, the group noticed an older couple crying over their son's grave. The Rabbi approached the couple*

and found out that they were the parents of a young man named Erez Deri, who was killed in action in 2006. Mrs. Deri said that her son had come to her in a dream the night before and asked her to dedicate a Sefer Torah in his name. This, he said, would take the place of the chuppah he never had. Her son also told her to visit his grave the next day, where she would find good people who would help raise money to write the Torah.

Rabbi Eliach had no doubt that he and his group were the "good people" to whom Erez was referring. The group agreed to raise the money needed for the project and promised that in one year, they would return with a new Sefer Torah written in Erez's merit. True to their word, they returned exactly one year later. The sofer wrote the last letters of the Torah at the Deri home, on the desk that had belonged to Erez. The celebration was like a wedding, filled with simchah, music, and dancing.

At last, Erez's parents found comfort for their loss. The Sefer Torah would bring their son continuous merit, and the kindness of their fellow Jews would forever warm their hearts.

MAKE IT REAL:

Whether your situation is one in which you have the opportunity to give, or you are in need of help, think of the tests each situation involves and choose to fill your role in the best way possible.

72

Before and After

When we pray, things change.

We can be sure that we will not get through life — or probably even a week — without something happening that will upset us. What should we do with that feeling? Most people respond one of two ways. Either they become sad and lose their energy, or they become angry and look for someone to blame. If they choose one of those options and go no further, then they've not only suffered the setback, but lost the opportunity it could have given them to come a bit closer to Hashem through a sincere *tefillah*.

By steering ourselves in the direction of *tefillah* instead of uselessly letting depression or anger take hold, we show ourselves and Hashem that we know Who runs the world. Not only do we recognize that Hashem created and controls the world, but also, that He is the only Source of help for whatever it is that we need at that moment.

One time, Rav Dessler asked the Chazon Ish a question about *tefillah*. He wanted to know why, after we begin *Shemoneh Esrei* with spiritual requests for wisdom, closeness to Hashem, forgiveness and redemption, we then sink back into the worldly needs of *parnassah* and *refuah*. Why do we start with such lofty ideas and then come down the ladder into the worries of daily life?

The answer that the Chazon Ish gave Rav Dessler teaches us that what seems like a come-down is actually a climb to the peak of *emunah*. With the first requests in *Shemoneh Esrei,* we remind ourselves that Hashem controls everything. We then apply that *emunah* to the challenges we face in our life. By praying to Hashem to heal someone who is sick, we recognize that doctors and medicine are helpless without Hashem's healing power. When we pray for *parnassah,* we confirm that the money we earn isn't the result of our work; only Hashem can turn our work into a livelihood.

Coming to Hashem with real conviction that we are going straight to the Source of everything we need fulfills the Torah's mitzvah of *emunah*. "This is the foundation of all other mitzvos," said the Chazon Ish. "So those two *berachos* are very powerful."

The Gemara (*Rosh Hashanah* 18a) tells of two men suffering from the same serious illness. One recovers and the other passes away. Explaining why the men's fates were so different from each other, the Gemara says that while both men prayed, the one who survived prayed a *tefillah sheleimah* — a complete prayer, which Rashi defines as prayer with *kavannah*. We might wonder how a person who is dying could lack *kavannah* as he prays for his recovery, and Rav Elyah Lopian explains it: Certainly they both prayed with concentration, but the one who didn't survive did not believe that his prayers would change his situation. He was praying "just in case" it might work. The man who recovered, on the other hand, knew that he was using the most powerful tool in existence to help himself (*Praying With Fire 2*, Rabbi Heshy Kleinman).

A sincere prayer contains all our trust in Hashem. We are coming to Him not like someone who is going door to door hoping to receive a donation, but like someone going to exactly the right address, where he knows a huge check is waiting for him. Such a prayer changes reality, as this story from Rabbi Elimelech Biderman illustrates:

> *Rabbi Nechemia Baker was 26 when his wife gave birth to their first child. The baby was healthy, but Mrs. Baker's recovery did not go smoothly. Her doctor said that surgery was necessary to save her life. He also informed her that after the surgery, she would no longer be able to have children.*

Rabbi Baker went to ask the Chazon Ish's advice. "If it's a matter of life and death, of course you must do the surgery," he advised. However, since it was Minchah time, he asked Rabbi Baker to stay for davening and they would speak again afterward. When they met after davening, the Chazon Ish told him to cancel the operation. Everything would be fine.

"But you just said that without question, the surgery should be done," Rabbi Baker answered in surprise.

"That was before Minchah," the Chazon Ish explained. "Now it is after Minchah. Tefillah has the power to change nature."

The couple followed the Chazon Ish's advice and Mrs. Baker lived to the ripe old age of 88. She had an additional nine children, and one of them told Rabbi Biderman this story.

MAKE IT REAL:

Tefillah and emunah go hand-in-hand, each strengthening the other. Choose one request that you make of Hashem during Shemoneh Esrei and focus on saying a "tefillah sheleimah."

73

You're Good As New

Sleep is one of Hashem's greatest gifts.

It's 9 p.m. at your neighbor's wedding. The *chassan's* five-year-old nephew is clinging to his mother's gown whining, "Pick me u-u-u-p." His mother can't do it; the boy is too heavy for her to carry around. Even so, he holds on to her skirt wherever she goes, whimpering and whining. "He's tired," the mother explains to a friend. "He should have been in bed two hours ago."

Children become cranky when they don't sleep. Adults do, too. They have less patience, less ability to concentrate, and less enthusiasm. Their brain is whining and whimpering, "Just leave me alone and let me get some rest!" In fact, purposely depriving a person of sleep for an extended period of time is considered a form of torture.

When we try to think about and appreciate the everyday gifts Hashem has put into our world, we often focus on the food we eat, the air we breathe, and the wonder of our body. Sleep seldom makes it onto our thank-you list, but it should, because without sleep, our food wouldn't interest us and our body and mind would quickly wear down.

Think of this amazing process. Every night, we lose awareness of the world around us for somewhere around eight hours. We do not hear the people talking in the next room or the creaking of the floor or the rain and wind banging against the window. Moreover, our minds create an entirely different reality, producing complicated fantasies that play out in our dreams. Most of us could never come up with such vivid tales in our waking hours.

While we lie there removed from reality, Hashem is giving our bodies a tune-up, a cleaning and a recharging all at once. One important benefit is sleep's effect on our memory. Researchers have discovered that while we sleep, our brain transfers information we have learned from the "short term" to the "long term" storage area. Another vital process that takes place when we sleep is the release of growth hormones into our bloodstream. During the years in which a person is growing to his adult height, a lack of sleep can slow down the process and even limit the person's height. Throughout adult life, these same hormones play an important role in maintaining healthy weight and energy.

And there's much more. Sleep-time is when the body's cells recharge. It's when the liver rebuilds itself and processes all the toxins it has been busy removing from our blood throughout the day. The immune system also becomes stronger during sleep because of proteins and antibodies our body releases during that time. This is what helps us fight infections and enables us to heal faster when we do become ill. In addition to these benefits, people who get enough sleep have fewer problems with cholesterol, blood pressure, obesity, and diabetes. You can only imagine the number of medications and treatments that would be necessary to accomplish all of this, and yet all we have to do is lay our head down on our pillow, close our eyes, and drift into dreamland.

While our body is being rebalanced and renewed, our soul experiences the gift of sleep on an entirely different level. As we know, Hashem takes a part of the soul back to *Shamayim* every night and returns it to us faithfully each morning. When we say *Modeh Ani* in the morning, we recognize that He, in His unlimited kindness, has given us a new day of life even though we may have sinned the previous day. Each day He gives us a new opportunity to achieve, improve, repair any wrongs, and serve Him a little better.

Rachel knew that she shouldn't worry about her seminary applications. She had done her best to choose good options and make a good impression. Now it was up to Hashem, or at least that's what her mind was saying. Her body, however, couldn't let go of the stress. Every night, she woke up from her sleep and tossed and turned for hours. She fell back to sleep for a short while and then the alarm clock rang. Her eyes were sticky, her body heavy as she mumbled Modeh Ani and started her day.

When at last she received her first acceptance letter, she felt a flood of relief. That night, she fell into a deep, dream-filled sleep. Nothing disturbed her until her alarm clock rang at seven a.m. the next morning. She realized with a surge of gratitude that she had just enjoyed her first good night's sleep in months. So soundly had she slept that her blanket had barely shifted from the position it was in eight hours earlier.

Rachel sat up. Her eyes were clear and her limbs full of energy. That morning, she said "Modeh Ani" with a whole new feeling.

MAKE IT REAL:

When you say Modeh Ani, keep in mind that your soul has just returned from Shamayim and your body has just emerged good as new from the repair shop.

74

Be That Person

Emunah is the tool that repairs all our middos.

Think of someone you consider a really good person — someone everyone likes and wants as a friend. He's a person you can always count on for a favor, the first one you want to tell when you've got good news to share, and the one you can turn to for support when the going gets tough.

What makes him this way? "He was born this way," you might think. "He's had an easygoing personality since he was in kindergarten."

You'd be correct in saying that some people have a calmer nature. However, anyone can get there. In fact, everyone has *middos* that need improvement. The Vilna Gaon (*Mishlei* 4:13) teaches that building our positive traits and breaking our negative inclinations is the very purpose of our life. Therefore, Hashem fills our days with opportunities to get to work.

Many things happen in the course of a day that kick off a "gut reaction," which is our first instinct. These reactions are our instinctive *middos* rushing to the front of our mind, trying to tell us what to do. Someone wants your help? Your natural laziness says, "I don't have time." Someone borrows your dress and spills grape juice on it? Your natural anger says, "How could you be so careless?" You're stuck in traffic? Your natural impatience says, "Lean on the horn!" Someone receives the award you believe you deserve? Your natural envy says, "It's not fair!"

The one tool you possess that can repair all these natural inclinations is *emunah*. It is the only force strong enough to silence that negative voice. You may still hear the voice, but you can quickly answer it, "Hashem runs the world. *Gam zu l'tovah.*" Eventually, the voice will become nothing more than a whisper, or it may disappear altogether. The more you work on *emunah,* the more your *middos* will improve. By taming your jealousy, anger, impatience, and laziness, you will become "that person" — the one everyone wants as a friend.

You will at the same time be accomplishing exactly what Hashem sent you here to accomplish. In this world, you'll have a calm and happy life. In the next world, you'll have the reward of all your efforts — a great *avodah* that you undertook day after day. Sometimes, as in the true story below, Hashem will show you just how much He treasures that *avodah.*

> *Twenty-five years ago, a Rabbi from Brooklyn and his wife and daughter were waiting in an airport in Toronto for a return flight home. He had booked a Sunday night flight so that he could be home in time for a meeting on Monday morning, and his daughter could be on time for school. However, when they reached the gate, the airline agent told them that they had been bumped from the flight.*
>
> *Unable to get an explanation from the agent, the Rabbi was becoming quite upset. His wife quietly reminded him that he would make a chillul Hashem if he became angry in public, and he regained his self-control. The agent brought the family to a new waiting area where they were to get on a flight scheduled for a half-hour after the original one. It would land in New York instead of Newark, where their luggage had already been sent.*
>
> *At that gate, another agent told them that the new flight was full and they would not be able to board. The Rabbi calmly asked to see a supervisor. As he waited, he noticed a crumpled garment bag nearby. It seemed familiar to him. When he looked closer, he realized that it was his. Inside were two new suits and all his wife's hanging clothes, which they had apparently forgotten.*

Now he realized that Hashem had saved them from losing this expensive clothing.

When the manager came, he told them that they would be allowed on the flight. Furthermore, the airline's rule was to reimburse bumped passengers for their inconvenience; the manager handed the Rabbi $600 in cash. With his recovered garment bag and unexpected cash gift, the Rabbi and his family boarded the plane. Just then, a flight attendant came to tell them that their luggage, which would be landing in Newark, would be delivered to their home in Brooklyn. Furthermore, the airline would pay for the car service between the airport and the family's home.

The Rabbi later recounted that "The delay that almost caused me to explode was actually a chesed from Hashem." Instead of making a scene, he reminded himself that Hashem was in charge; he never imagined that his lost luggage, $600 and car-service fare would be his instant reward.

MAKE IT REAL:

When you hear the voice of negative instincts, use your emunah to "talk back."

75

What's the Real Deal?

Seeking a zechus, we find a mitzvah.

A girl comes home from seminary; first on her to-do list is to find a job. She begins her search full of optimism, sending her resume to dozens of businesses that are advertising for help. As the weeks go by, she gets only two responses to her resume and neither of them work out. One night as she tries to fall asleep, she ponders her situation and decides to take on an added mitzvah as a *zechus* to draw from *Shamayim* the help that she needs.

"Maybe I need to help my mother more," she thinks. "Maybe Hashem is telling me, 'You're not even doing the job you already have. Why should I give you another job?' For sure that's it!"

The next morning, she launches into her new helpful mode. She helps her younger siblings get ready for school and takes the baby out for a walk while her mother gets ready for work. The girl's eyes begin to focus on the needs of others in her family rather than thinking only of her own needs. On Wednesday of that week, she is invited to be interviewed for a job. On Thursday, the owner of the business calls to offer her the position. In this girl's view, her strategy worked; she took on a mitzvah as a merit and Hashem rewarded her with the job.

What she doesn't realize, however, is that she has it backward. Hashem denied her a job for all those weeks to push her to look in the mirror, figure out what she could be doing better, and do it. The *chesed* and *kibbud eim* she performed for her mother — not the job — was her real "win."

Hashem is always focused on our spiritual growth. He withholds or gives us material blessings only to prod us to new heights of *tefillah, teshuvah,* Torah learning, and mitzvos. We always have the free choice to use our challenges in the right way, or to close our ears to Hashem's voice and see the situation as bad luck. If we choose to improve ourselves in order to earn the merit we're seeking, then even if we don't receive the answer to our dilemma, we come out ahead. We've grown spiritually and come closer to Hashem. To say, "I learned an extra 10 minutes a day and it got me nowhere!" is to miss the entire point.

A True Story

Aaron wondered what was wrong with his voice. It had become so hoarse, and it was becoming painful just to speak. He went to a top doctor in Manhattan to find out what was wrong. The doctor found a small growth called a polyp on Aaron's vocal cord. "How did that ever happen?" Aaron wondered. "Usually it's people who use their voice a lot, like singers, who get polyps." Not only did he not sing or even speak much in public, but his natural speaking voice was soft.

Despite the mystery, there was only one solution. Aaron needed surgery to remove the polyp. He scheduled it for a month from his appointment. Meanwhile, as a thinking Jew, Aaron followed the Gemara's advice to try to find the spiritual flaw that might have caused the physical problem. "OK, so if it has to do with my voice, then obviously I have to think about how I speak," he reasoned. "But I really do not speak lashon hara. I try to be so careful. What else could it be?"

A likely answer entered his mind. When Aaron's wife spoke to him, he had a bad habit of interrupting her and cutting her off. He was so eager to add his own insight that he didn't let his wife finish her story or her thought. She had even spoken to him about this habit in the past and he had to admit that nothing had changed.

Aaron approached his wife and apologized for his interruptions. "From today," he said, "I am making a commitment to give you my full attention and not interrupt you or anyone else who is talking."

On the day of Aaron's surgery, he arrived early at the doctor's office. He asked the doctor to examine his throat again to make certain that the polyp was still there. The doctor laughed and told him, "Polyps don't disappear on their own." However, he did what Aaron asked and double-checked his condition. To his amazement, for the first time in his 30 years of practice, he encountered a polyp that did disappear. When he asked Aaron how he managed to accomplish this, Aaron answered simply, "I prayed."

Aaron took upon himself to be an attentive, respectful listener when others — especially his wife — spoke to him. He did it in an effort to cure the spiritual flaw that was causing the physical disease, and he succeeded. However, his real prize was not that the polyp went away on his own, but that he became a better person — and that was Hashem's purpose all along.

MAKE IT REAL:

When you take on a mitzvah as a merit to bring about a certain result, remember that whether you get your result or not, you have accomplished your real purpose.

76

When Hashem Says "I Love You" Loud and Clear

There are moments that make emunah easy.

Usually, building *emunah* is hard work. We have to be alert for our reaction when something doesn't go our way and yank our negative thoughts and anger onto another track. When a future event has us worried, we have to keep reassuring ourselves that Hashem will help us, and that whatever the outcome might be, it's the outcome that is best for us. This is difficult to do when one of the possible outcomes is painful. It is also difficult to do when we want a particular result very badly. The only answer in these situations is to work on making Hashem a reality for ourselves — and even that takes plenty of focus and effort, because He hides Himself in our world.

One of the most wonderful occurrences in life is when Hashem brings about something we've been waiting and praying for in a way that is so improbable that it could only have come from Him. At that moment, we don't have to work hard at all. Hashem is stepping out of the shadows, sending us a clear, loving message that says, "Here, this is for you. It's just what you asked for." We feel that we actually "see" Him and we're amazed.

When a couple becomes engaged, this is often the feeling they have. If they come from places or circumstances that are very different from each other, they might say, "Who else but Hashem could have put us together?" If they grew up around the corner from each other, they think, "Hashem put my *bashert* right in front of me. All I had to do was look!" One of the reasons that *shidduchim* are compared to the splitting of the *Yam Suf* is because like that miracle, *shidduchim* clearly reveal the workings of *Shamayim*.

When Hashem shows His hand, so to speak, our hearts fill with excitement. This powerful reminder that Hashem is right here, listening to our prayers and directing our life, allows us to feel His love in the most direct and uplifting way. It makes us think, "How could I ever have doubted? The proof is right here in front of me!"

The more we experience these moments, the more easily we will be able to tap into our *emunah* to deal with difficulties. The question that whispers in the back of a person's brain, "How do I know Hashem will help me?" fades over time because our experiences teach us that we have a loving Father in Heaven, Whom we can trust. Growing in our *emunah* takes work, but every so often, Hashem gives us a powerful boost. We need only take notice and make sure we don't forget His act of wondrous kindness.

In the summer of 2006, war broke out between Israel and a terrorist group in Northern Lebanon, but Yaakov Salber stuck with his plan to visit Eretz Yisrael. He was going to stay with relatives in Har Nof, far from the action, and he was bringing them a beautiful silver mezuzah as a gift.

As he traveled from the airport in his rental car, he spotted a group of soldiers hitching at the side of the road. He pulled over and asked if any of them were heading to Har Nof. One boy, Menachem, climbed in, grateful to be out of the sweltering heat. His unit was going into Lebanon the next day and he was on his way home to say goodbye to his parents.

When the young soldier got out of the car in Har Nof, Yaakov called him to come back. He reached into his carry-on and pulled out the silver mezuzah. "Keep this in your pocket," he told Menachem. "Keep it there all the time. And when you come back, we'll hang it together."

Menachem was deeply touched. He told Yaakov that

his older brother had been killed as a soldier in a raid on a terrorist stronghold, and with that loss, his father lost his faith. When they moved into their present apartment, no mezuzos were hung. Menachem tucked the mezuzah in his pocket and turned toward his parents' home.

All summer, Yaakov prayed for Menachem and followed news of the war, listening intently when names of fallen soldiers were announced. Then one day, he heard the news he was dreading — Menachem had been killed. After procrastinating for a few days, he finally got up the courage to pay Menachem's parents a shivah call. Strangely, it seemed that a party was going on. Menachem's father greeted him with a smile and brought him to Menachem's bedroom, where, to Yaakov's utter shock, the soldier was lying in bed recovering from a bullet wound to his leg.

He had been mistaken for dead, but was only unconscious. He had been shot in the leg and the heart. "How did you survive?" Yaakov asked him. Menachem reached into his pocket and pulled out the mezuzah. Embedded in it was a single bullet. Menachem and Yaakov hung the mezuzah, bullet and all, while his father, his faith miraculously restored, stood silently weeping (Stories for the Jewish Heart, Book 2, Rabbi Binyamin Pruzansky).

MAKE IT REAL:

Write down the moments when you or someone you know has an experience in which Hashem "shows His hand" clearly. Read these notes once in a while to remind yourself that Hashem loves us.

77

Don't let the good become background music.

Let's ask a simple question: Why does it seem so much harder for people to notice the hundreds of gifts Hashem sends them each day than the one or two things that go wrong? Why does the good turn into background music that we barely notice, while the challenges sound like a 100-decibel wedding band?

Rabbi Fischel Schachter tells a story that illustrates exactly how difficult it can be to get people to think about the Source of the good that comes their way:

> *There was a successful businessman who had just finished a major, high-pressure meeting. Matters had gone well and he was feeling on top of the world. Since his office was on a high floor of a skyscraper, he decided to relieve his stress and celebrate his success by spending a few minutes on the rooftop, with its breathtaking view of the city.*
>
> *He took the elevator to the top floor and walked through a doorway onto the roof. The breeze blew the door shut and the businessman, suddenly feeling a sense of foreboding, tried to reopen the door. It was locked. What would he do? As this was in the times before cell phones, he had no way to let anyone know he was stranded. The hour was getting late, the air was turning cold, and the man didn't know how long it would be*

before anyone even looked for him.

He tried yelling down to the street, but it was futile. There was no way his voice could carry all that distance. Then he remembered that he had a collection of rare coins in his briefcase. He took one and threw it down onto the crowded sidewalk below; it hit a passerby. The man picked up the coin, shrugged at his good luck, put it in his pocket, and walked on. "Maybe the next guy will look up and wonder where the coin came from," the businessman thought. He threw yet another coin, which fell in front of another passerby, but he too pocketed his lucky coin and walked on.

After tossing a few more coins and getting the same reaction, the businessman grew frustrated. Why didn't anyone look up to see where the coins were coming from? Did they think it was raining money? "I might as well just throw a rock," he decided. He found a small rock and hurled it toward the street. It hit a pedestrian on the arm and fell to the sidewalk in front of him. The man instantly grabbed the rock and looked up to the building. "Hey! Who's throwing rocks?" he shouted. People around him looked up too, and one of them spotted the businessman waving his arms from the rooftop. The police were called and soon, the relieved businessman was explaining himself to the two officers, who accepted the man's explanation.

Rabbi Schachter compared the pedestrians on the street to the average person. When good things fall upon us, we take them and walk on as if they were expected all along. When troubles strike, however, we look up accusingly at the One Who "did this to us."

Because good happenings don't prod us to look upward, even when Hashem's kindness hits us on the head, we have a false impression of the world. We think, "There are so many problems" when the reality is that Hashem's gifts far outweigh the problems. For example, you may know of an older single who is having trouble finding a *shidduch*. This person of course deserves our support, *tefillos,* and practical help, and we can be sure that Hashem has the very best reasons for the delay. However, none of this outweighs the kindness Hashem does in bringing thousands of couples together each year. Nor does it outweigh the myriad kindnesses He does for the person who is awaiting a *shidduch*. Likewise, your own family or someone you know might be having financial troubles, yet Hashem is no less the One Who sustains every form of life that He has created, each according to its needs. Coins don't really fall from the sky!

How does it help to know that Hashem is kind when we, in our own situation, are not experiencing the kindness we feel that we need? It helps by enabling us to trust Him. We realize that whatever we are experiencing must also be kindness, even though we do not understand it. If we trust Him, we can go where He takes us without fear or worry.

MAKE IT REAL:

This week, before you daven, think of one unique kindness Hashem has done for you personally. Think of that kindness as you bow to say Modim.

78

We Don't Notice the Music

Hashem is prodding us to turn our eyes back to Him.

Have you ever been to a *simchah* where there is background music playing? It's not loud dance music meant to get people up on their feet. It's just pleasant, calm music meant to create a nice atmosphere while the guests eat and talk to each other. Most people don't notice the music. But then, it stops — it's time for the *chassan* and *kallah* to come in or for the bar mitzvah boy to speak. The silence when the music stops is often "louder" than the music itself. Why?

The reason is that when something is always present, we stop noticing it. Even the most wonderful thing we can imagine loses its "wow!" when we become used to it. What we do notice, very clearly, is when it vanishes. A person doesn't normally notice how wonderful it is to stand, walk, and run, but if he breaks his leg, he suddenly realizes what a great gift two working legs are.

Because we forget to notice and be grateful for the gifts Hashem gives us, sometimes He withholds a certain gift. To us, it feels as if He is punishing us, but this is not the purpose. He is simply causing us to stop and appreciate what we have, just as we notice the beautiful music only when it stops playing. Hashem is grabbing our attention, prodding us to turn our eyes back to Him and realize that He is the One Who loves us and cares for our every need.

The best way to avoid having to learn gratitude by losing things is to learn it by appreciating things. If we teach ourselves to be grateful and notice our gifts, there is no need to "stop the music" to get our attention.

We can learn this from the Torah. When Miriam died (*Bamidbar* 20:1), the well of water that traveled through the Wilderness with the Jewish people dried up. Because the water had flowed in Miriam's merit, once she was gone, so was the water.

But it didn't have to be that way. The *Kli Yakar* says that the water would have been there for the Jewish people even after Miriam's death if they had appreciated her properly. When Moshe and Aharon died, the Torah tells us that *Klal Yisrael* mourned for them, but there is no mention of mourning when Miriam died. Therefore, the people needed to learn to appreciate what a great woman they had had among them. By removing the water, Hashem showed them that the water they had been drinking for the past 40 years was all in Miriam's merit. Today, Hashem is once again sending the message to appreciate what we had loud and clear to *Klal Yisrael*.

> *In March 2020, the Covid-19 virus caused something the world had never seen before — a total world-wide lockdown. Nearly every business closed and people everywhere were warned to stay in their own homes. No one was allowed to have guests for Pesach — not even married children and grandchildren. There were no simchos, no minyanim, schools and yeshivos were all locked up tight.*
>
> *Suddenly, all the simple everyday activities of the "old way of life" seemed to belong to a long-ago magical time when everything was possible. Yet the "old days" were only a few months earlier. Why did the world seem so different from before? Not because it was a new decade or a new century, but only because it was a new point of view. Suddenly, we truly realized how very much we had, not so long ago.*

MAKE IT REAL:

Write down five ways Hashem shows you that He loves you every day.

79

If You Know the Child, You Know the Father

We feel Hashem's kindness through other Jews.

You take a job as a camp counselor. You have one camper who is especially kind and friendly. You notice that she is always the first to lend items of clothing to her bunkmates and that she makes a point of spending time with one particularly homesick girl. When conflicts begin to brew, she is the one to make peace. When she gets a package of goodies from home, she gives most of it away.

When visiting day comes, a couple approaches you and with warm smiles, they thank you for giving their daughter a wonderful summer. Then they hand you a generous tip. You are not a bit surprised to discover that they are the parents of this special girl, because they exude the same sweet, warm personality as their daughter.

We can often sense what a person's parents are like just by knowing the child. After all, most children emulate their parents; if they're kind and giving, we can assume that their parents are, as well.

When a Jew acts as a Jew should, according to the traits the Torah teaches, he becomes the kind of child through whom we can recognize his Father. This is especially true when a Jew does an act of kindness. The Gemara (*Sotah* 14a) tells us that the Torah begins and ends with kindness. In *Bereishis,* Hashem makes clothing for Adam and Chava; in *Zos HaBerachah,* He buries Moshe Rabbeinu. From this, we learn that Hashem loves to bestow kindness on us. We, His children, fulfill the mitzvah to emulate Him by performing acts of kindness for each other.

This is why, when someone steps in and helps us out when we need it, we experience it as a "hug from Hashem." We realize that it is He Who led us to this particular person in order to send us the help we need. We sense that our fellow Jews are Hashem's children, acting toward us as our Father would wish.

Because kindness enables us to "act like Hashem," the nature of a Jew is to seek ways to help others. We not only do *chesed,* but we are meant to love *chesed* and look for opportunities to do it. As we say in *Sim Shalom* at the close of *Shemoneh Esrei,* "You gave us, L-rd our G-d, the Torah of life and the love of *chesed*, righteousness, blessing, compassion, life, and peace." When we fulfill this potential that is in us, we not only emulate Hashem, but also, we give the person receiving our kindness the incomparable feeling that Hashem is taking care of him.

A TRUE STORY

Yerucham Klein decided to rent a bungalow in Upstate New York for his family during one of the last weeks of summer, when most people had already gone back to the city. After a stressful year, it seemed like just what they needed.*

Yerucham drove his family to the bungalow and got a ride back to the city. He planned to work during the week and get another ride back to the country for Shabbos. However, things did not work out as expected. The Kleins' baby developed a bad cough and Mrs. Klein had to bring him to the doctor several times. Finally, on Thursday, she brought her son to the emergency room. The baby was able to go home after being treated for his cough, but Mrs. Klein had no time to shop for Shabbos.

When she spoke to her husband that night, she told him that she had nothing for Shabbos — not even challah and grape juice. However, because of a bad cell phone connection, he mistook her to say that she had everything but challah and grape juice. He arrived in the country empty-handed, thinking he would pick up those two items in a local store. Instead, he had to run out just an hour and a half before candle-lighting to try to scrounge up food for an entire Shabbos. Worse yet, his GPS connection failed and he lost his way on the long, winding country roads.

At this point, there was only one place to turn for help, and so he recited some Tehillim and said a simple, heart-felt prayer: "Hashem, help me!" He then decided to turn onto a different road, which brought him right to the front of Machaneh Bnos Belz girls' camp. He saw a chassidic man at the gate, who informed him that no stores remained open. When Yerucham told the man his sad story, the chassid directed him to the camp kitchen. There, he was given everything from gefilte fish to dessert. He even received a spelt challah for his allergic child.

When he tried to pay the kitchen manager for the food, the manager told him, "Here in Belz, that's what we're about — helping a fellow Jew in need. We're not taking your money."

Yerucham later said that when he tells this story, it brings tears to his eyes. "Hashem guided me to the exact place I needed to be to get help." Through the chesed-loving Jews at the Belzer girls' camp, Yerucham felt Hashem's kindness.

MAKE IT REAL:

When someone is kind to you, remember that he's acting just like his Father.

80

The Cure Comes Before the Illness

It's just what you need, just when you need it!

People can live without much money. They can live with poor health. They can even live locked up in prison. The one thing they cannot live without for long is hope. As unscientific as it might seem, hope has been proven to help sick people heal and help elderly people live longer. When we're going through a difficult time, hope is what keeps us going and gives us strength to tackle the challenge. Once we say, "What's the use?" the game is over.

A pessimist, however, sees hope as a fantasy, as if the hopeful person believes in magic. He would rather "face reality" and live in gloom than hold on to the belief that his troubles will one day vanish. He believes that in this way, he saves himself from disappointment, failing to realize that by shutting down his hopes, he's turning his whole life into a disappointment. Where is Hashem's love and care in his picture of life? It's nowhere to be seen.

If we would only look inside the Torah and Tanach, we would see that Hashem is telling us in hundreds of ways to never lose hope in His salvation. Although these holy *sefarim* seem to be filled with the history of our people, the purpose of all these stories is to teach us Who Hashem is and how He deals with His children. Over and over, He shows us that the most hopeless situation can flip on its head in a moment.

For example, why does the Torah present us with three of

the *Imahos* who struggled to have children? One purpose is to tell us that we must keep praying for Hashem to grant us what we need no matter how many *tefillos* we have already prayed. In a similar way, the Torah relates the seemingly hopeless situation of Yosef HaTzaddik, who was thrown in the dungeon and forgotten. Meanwhile, events transpired in Pharaoh's palace that led to Yosef being unexpectedly plucked from his cell and appointed as Pharaoh's most trusted advisor.

The Purim story is another account that shouts to us, "It can all change in an instant!" In fact, one of this *chag's* central themes is "*V'nahafoch hu*" — everything is turned upside down. One moment, the Jewish people throughout the Persian Empire are in mourning, their day of doom written and sealed with the king's signet ring. The next moment, the Jews are honored, their enemies are killed, and the same signet ring that sealed their doom is given to Mordechai.

In all these instances, Hashem has already assembled the necessary components so that at the right moment, the situation will miraculously be resolved. Had Esther not been selected as queen before Haman's decree was issued, she would not have been in a position to advocate for her people. Had Pharaoh not dreamed his troubling dream, Yosef would not have been released from prison. We cannot know what events Hashem is planning behind the scenes. We only need to know that everything required to solve our troubles is already in place, as the following true story illustrates.

A TRUE STORY

Chaim lived in Monroe, N.Y., where he volunteered for Hatzolah. As the yahrtzeit of Rebbe Yeshayah of Kerestir approached, he found himself longing to daven at his kever in Hungary. Chaim had never done such a thing before, but his heart urged him to go. At such short notice, the earliest flight he was able to book was scheduled for the day of the yahrtzeit, but he calculated that he would still get there in time to reach the grave before evening.*

His plan depended on everything running smoothly; Hashem had other plans. Once Chaim landed in Hungary, it took him an hour to find a driver. Then, as the driver zoomed along the highway, a horrific traffic accident happened right in front of his car. The driver slammed on the brakes and Chaim jumped out of the car to see if he could be of help. He saw two Jewish boys lying unconscious on the road. Using his Hatzolah skills, he performed CPR, alternating from one boy to the other for 15 minutes until an ambulance came. He saved both of their lives.

Only a few days before, Chaim had no thoughts of going to Reb Yeshayah's grave. It would never have occurred to him, but for some reason, this year it did. Added to that unlikely occurrence, he had to search for an hour for a driver. It all added up to a trained EMT being in exactly the right place at exactly the right time to save two Jewish lives.

Hashem knows how to bring salvation and He directs our steps accordingly, but we have to do our part. For instance, the *Midrash* says that Hashem created the *Yam Suf* on the condition that it would part for the Jews leaving Egypt. However, it did not part until they rallied their *emunah* and jumped in. The salvation was there, but *emunah* was the ignition key that set it in motion.

MAKE IT REAL:

When a situation looks bleak, imagine the incredible joy of the Jews of Persia when they heard that they were saved. Remember it can all turn around in a moment.

81

Why Complain?

Save your complaints for the One Who can help.

You're standing on the check-out line at the supermarket. In front of you, a two-year-old sits in the front seat of his mother's shopping cart stretching out his hand for a candy bar on display. His mother says, "Sorry sweetie, not now. You've had enough candy today." The little boy starts whining, "I waaaant!" When that doesn't work, he starts screaming and kicking his little legs. His mother's efforts to quiet him down don't seem to have any effect. He didn't get what he wanted and he is going to let everyone in the store know how miserable he is.

Obviously, this is not mature behavior. Nevertheless, we should ask ourselves if at our own level, we are not sometimes just as unable to deal with "no." Whether it's something we want or something we need, when we cannot have it, we have two choices in front of us. One is to be a 12-year-old, 18-year-old, or even 50-year-old version of the little boy in the grocery store. The other is to follow the Gemara's advice (*Berachos* 63a) to "partner with Hashem" when we are in pain.

What does this mean? First of all, we have to realize that Hashem is already a partner with us. He is completely invested in our success and happiness; our gains are His gains, and our losses are His losses. Our pain is His pain, to a far greater degree than we can imagine. This is because His pain over our suffering is pure. Our own pain is usually a mixture of elements: the lack we feel, the impact it has on our self-image or other people's image of us, our anger at those who seem to be denying us, our worries about the future and so forth. Hashem sees only our need and desire, and He is pained that He cannot give us what we want at that moment, even though withholding it is for our good.

He cares for us and in our way, we must care for Him as well. The *Nefesh HaChaim* explains that when we have a complaint, letting everyone know about it can create a *chillul Hashem*. It's as if we are accusing Hashem of neglect or cruelty; He could help us in a flash, and yet He doesn't do so. As Hashem's partner, we should keep our business private. We should speak only to our Partner about what we need, rather than voicing to others our complaints about the way He runs things.

We all know people who answer, "How are you?" with a smile and a *"Baruch Hashem!"* no matter what is going on in their lives. Are they being dishonest? Not at all. We always have plenty about which to say, "*Baruch Hashem*." These blessings are the light in which such a person chooses to view his life. We also know people who answer, "How are you?" with a list of complaints. When things always seem to be going wrong in someone's life, people begin to wonder, "Why doesn't Hashem give this poor guy a break? It's one thing after another. How is anyone supposed to keep his head up with so much to deal with?" In other words, they think Hashem is picking on this person. Some people might even conclude that he deserves it. Either way, we can easily see that we do ourselves no favor by complaining.

Obviously, people do have serious challenges that they need to address with those who can help them. In that case, it is a mitzvah to seek help, speak honestly, and do everything necessary to resolve the issue. The point is to keep complaints out of our general conversations. Those who follow this path discover that they soon have far fewer reasons to complain.

> *A yeshivah boy named Bentzion was having a hard time with his learning. Since he had always been a successful student, his rebbi wondered what had changed. Then he found out. One day, Bentzion approached the rebbi as he sat in a quiet corner of the beis medrash.*

"Rebbi, I hate to say it, but I don't think Hashem wants my learning," the boy said.

He went on to describe several challenges that arose, one after another. His father had lost his job and now his plans to head to Eretz Yisrael after Succos were on hold. His 14-year-old brother, to whom he was very close, was heading in a bad direction. With all the difficulties, his parents were tense and worried, a mood that quickly spread throughout the family.

"So here's what I want to know," Bentzion said. "If Hashem wants my learning, why does He give me so many problems that I can't think straight? I just give up!"

The rebbi answered, "Bentzion, your learning is your avodas Hashem. But if you try not to complain, and instead just accept that for Hashem's good reasons, this is what your life has to be right now, that is the biggest avodas Hashem of all."

When we accept our challenges by facing them and working on them without complaining about them, we show Hashem that we trust Him as our partner. This can only bring good things into our life.

MAKE IT REAL:

When you hear yourself complaining, ask yourself if you are complaining to someone who can help, or are simply complaining.

82

Ask and Thank All Day

There is a simple formula for happiness and success.

"Say thank you."

It's one of the first things our parents teach us. Maybe that is because they know what a powerful effect those words have on the people who give to us and take care of us. A sincere "thank you" coming from the mouth of a sweet little child melts the heart and of course, motivates the giver to give more.

Unlike a human giver, Hashem does not need our thank-you. His "feelings" are not wounded when we slide along our day eating His food, breathing His air, using the incredible body He has given us, walking along His solid earth warmed by the rays of His sunshine — and give no thought to the One Who provides it all for us. The value of our thankfulness to Hashem is in what it does for us. This is why Chazal (*Berachos* 3:5) tell us that whatever happens in a person's life, "He should thank Hashem for it very, very much." This includes the events we wish would not have happened, because thanking Hashem in such circumstances shows that we believe He acts only for our good.

Naturally, Chazal also mean that we should thank Him for that which is clearly good in our eyes, the things that make us happy. Without question, we must thank Hashem for an open miracle; we learn from Chazal (*Midrash Tehillim* 18) that even though receiving a miracle "deducts from our account" of merit in the Next World, when we thank Hashem for the miracle, we not only lose nothing, but we gain forgiveness for our sins.

The *Shomer Emunim* (*Maamar Hashgachah Pratis* Ch. 23) takes this idea one step further. If we receive this great reward for thanking Hashem for open miracles, which we clearly see and easily appreciate, how much more is the reward for thanking Him for hidden miracles? Because hidden miracles are around us at all times, they comprise an open vault filled with merit, available for the taking. All we need to do is look around us and recognize the acts of kindness with which Hashem fills our life.

But even if a person doesn't feel motivated by merit that will come to him in the long term, when after 120 he reaches the Next World, he has so much to gain in this world, right now, by tuning himself in to a mindset of gratitude. It is the key to happiness and success, as we learn from Yosef HaTzaddik. The *Shomer Emunim* (ibid.) writes that Yosef constantly asked Hashem for help and thanked Him when he received it. "Whatever he did, Hashem made succeed in his hand," the Torah relates (*Bereishis* 39:3). This *pasuk* teaches us that by constantly keeping Hashem "in the loop," making Him the go-to Source for everything we need and the recipient of all our gratitude, we too can achieve success.

There is no better way to grow closer to Hashem than to notice what He does for us. When something works out for us, we thank Hashem. When someone helps us out, we thank him — and Hashem. When something doesn't work out for us, then, too, we can thank Hashem for leading us to face a challenge that will make us spiritually stronger. Our gratitude will always bring us blessing, as this scenario, based on a true story, illustrates:

> *It took Rivka four years to find a shidduch. That was because she was determined to marry a boy who was learning full-time in yeshivah, but her parents did not have much money to offer toward support. Rivka worked and saved, certain that eventually, she would find a boy to whom support was not an obstacle.*
>
> *She never thought bitter thoughts about her situation.*

Instead, she made sure to thank Hashem: for her job, which enabled her to earn money; for the time it was taking for her to find her bashert, which enabled her to save money; for her parents, who respected her wishes even while shadchanim told them that Rivka was being unrealistic. She even thanked Hashem for her chassan, who she knew was out there somewhere, waiting for the right moment to arrive.

One day, a neighbor called Rivka's mother and suggested a shidduch. "His name is Reuven. His mother is an old school friend I ran into recently. Her son is learning full-time and very into his learning. I asked if they were looking for support and she said, 'He doesn't believe in that. He says if it's the right girl, Hashem will work out the details.'"

Four weeks later, Rivka and Reuven were engaged. With Rivka's salary and a small contribution from her parents, they would get by. A few weeks after the vort, Reuven's kollel received a donation that enabled the married students to earn several hundred dollars more each month. "We're rich!" Rivka exclaimed. And in the truest sense, they were!

MAKE IT REAL:

Open a conversation with Hashem that continues throughout the day, whenever you have a few unoccupied moments. Thank Him for that which you are able to enjoy in the present, and then ask Him for whatever you need.

83

Your Lucky Day

Don't miss this special opportunity!

It's amazing — and it's true. There is a day Hashem has chosen for showering the world with unlimited kindness. Each of its 24 hours, each of its 1,440 minutes, will open opportunities for us unlike any we've had before and any we will have thereafter. We can use the special power of these moments to accomplish worlds of good; we can learn Torah with more focus than ever. Our prayers can be especially effective as we feel an unusually strong connection to our Father. We will sense that without a doubt, He is waiting to hear our requests and fulfill them.

Not only will this day give us special opportunities for serving Hashem, but it will also present us with unique opportunities for making our homes, schools, and neighborhoods happier, more peaceful places. On this amazing day, we'll feel a desire in our heart to forgive people with whom we are angry and to clear the air with people we've hurt or insulted in some way. We will have an unusually sharp eye for noticing the good in other people. Not only will we notice, but we'll feel motivated to tell them, just to make them feel special. Even if we've never thought of ourselves as "the type" to have a smile for everyone, today we will choose to be that type.

Additionally, on this day Hashem will place in front of us people who need the special knowledge or resources we have. The day before this, we may not have noticed them and by tomorrow, they might no longer need what we have to offer, but on this day, our *chesed* can make a difference in their life. On this day, we really count.

What an awesome day to anticipate! When we wake up on that morning, we will feel like the winner of a lottery, overwhelmed with excitement to get the day going. There's only one catch: Hashem's special offer lasts only 24 hours. There will be no other day like this special one that Hashem will give us. The opportunities we allow to pass us by will be gone for good. Therefore, the wise person will put his all into using this special day to its full advantage.

By now, you surely want to know, what is the day to which we are referring? What is the day that's especially opportune for Torah, *tefillah,* forgiveness, kind words, *chesed,* and *shalom*?

That day is today — and every day to come.

Every day, Hashem gives us a new menu of opportunities. It has never been before and will never be again. Once the moments pass, they are gone for good, but each of them is open and waiting for us to fill with kindness to others and connection to Hashem. He shines His light on every moment of every day, lighting up each bit of time like a precious diamond. When we learn to treasure each "gem of a moment" as its own gift from Hashem, our life becomes vastly more productive and rewarding.

> *When Covid-19 hit the world, Avraham's yeshivah was forced to close. He and his chavrusa, Binyamin, decided to learn together by telephone. At first, they were determined to make the most of the situation. They had a fighting spirit: "We're going to show Hashem that no matter what, we'll do everything to keep learning full strength," Avraham thought to himself as he dialed Binyamin's phone number on the first day of their "remote beis medrash."*
>
> *As the days and weeks turned into months, their focus faded. They missed the atmosphere of the beis medrash with its noise and energy. Two guys on a phone just couldn't carry the day. As the learning grew dull, Avraham's mind began to wander. The boys found*

themselves schmoozing about Covid, the upcoming elections, dating during the lockdown, and many other topics that suddenly seemed very important.

Gradually, Avraham realized that he was becoming sluggish. With no place to go and nothing to do, he spent most of his time texting friends, reading magazines, and lazily helping around the house when his parents asked. With so little energy expended by day, he found it hard to sleep at night, which only sapped his energy further.

One day, he heard that a friend's father was seriously sick with Covid, lying in the hospital on a ventilator. That night as Avraham tried to fall asleep, his mind kept returning to his friend's father. "One day he's running a big business and the next day he's stuck in bed trying to breathe," he thought. He felt a sudden twist of panic in his stomach. Who said his life would be long? Who said he had decades more to get things done? The dreary, wasteful hours of the past few months looked like the height of foolishness now. But he realized that panic was not the answer; a schedule filled with purposeful activities, real goals, and real plans was the answer. The next day, he created a schedule for his day. It included his learning seder, another sefer he had wanted to learn, phone calls and offers to run errands for older relatives, fix-it projects in his house, exercise, and some time for playing his guitar. At the end of Day One, he climbed into bed tired and satisfied. For the first time in months, he slept soundly and woke up excited to start his day. There was so much to be done!

MAKE IT REAL:

Write down a list of things you know you should do but never get around to. Schedule them into your week with a specific day and time.

84

How Do We Love Hashem?

It's a two-way promise.

The Torah tells us how Hashem wants us to love Him: "*b'chol levave'cha uv'chol nafshecha uv'chol me'odecha* — With all your heart, with all your soul, and with all your resources" (*Devarim* 6:5). This is a tall order. It means that no matter what it costs us — in pain, in money, even in our life — our love for Hashem remains firm. We are like soldiers who have enlisted in a king's army, promising that we will serve him with "everything we've got."

Imagine if a human being were to say to us, "You must promise that no matter what I ask of you, you'll accept it with love. Even if it hurts you. Even if you don't understand it." How would we ever agree to such a demand? We would only agree if this complete devotion went both ways.

This is why we recite "*Ahavas olam ahavtanu* — With eternal love You have loved us," before we recite the above words from *Devarim* in the first paragraph of the *Shema*. Hashem's love for us can never be shaken. It will never fade. No matter what, He will always act for our benefit. He shows this to us in everything He does, in every breath we take and every moment of life He gives us. Knowing this, we can promise our unconditional love in return.

If the king's soldier is loyal and believes that the king is fair and good to his subjects, he doesn't become angry at the king when he faces a tough battle against an enemy. Instead, he sees it as a chance to show his courage and loyalty. Likewise, we can accept our challenges as an opportunity to show Hashem how much we really love Him. Rabbi Akiva taught us the ultimate level of love for Hashem when, as the Romans tortured him to death, he said the *Shema* and proclaimed that he was grateful to have finally been able to prove he truly did love Hashem "with all his soul."

When life becomes difficult, we, too, have a chance to dig deep into ourselves and find our unconditional love for Hashem. Whether it's our time, money, convenience, success in achieving something we want, health or any other challenge, when we accept it with love, we no longer feel abandoned.

A TRUE STORY

Yinon was a soldier in the IDF. At one point, he was with his unit learning how to operate anti-tank missiles. Because he kept falling asleep during his sergeant's lecture, the sergeant ordered him to stand guard outside. However, Yinon didn't want to leave. He said he would stand throughout the lecture to prevent himself from falling asleep.

Then tragedy struck. Accidentally, the sergeant set off the missile and it severed both of Yinon's legs. For months, he lay in bed devastated by his misfortune. At only 21 years old, he had a whole life ahead of him, but what would his future be? He was angry at Hashem, angry at the sergeant, and angry at himself for not leaving when he was told to do so.

Eventually, however, he was given artificial legs and learned how to use them. He was able to live a normal life, and even married. He began to accept that what happened had been part of Hashem's plan, and could have been much worse. Had he remained seated, the explosion would have killed him.

In fact, Yinon realized that Hashem was protecting him even then, because the missile struck right beneath the strings of his longest tzitzis. He had always told his fellow (non-religious) soldiers that his tzitzis were his "shield," and indeed they were. Now, instead of living with bitterness, Yinon travels the world telling of Hashem's kindness. Holding on to his love for Hashem enables him to feel Hashem's love in return.

It isn't easy to feel love for Hashem in difficult times, but when we do, we give ourselves the most powerful vaccine against despair. Whether or not we receive the help we're hoping for, just saying "I love you Hashem" in a time of trouble earns us phenomenal rewards.

MAKE IT REAL:

Is there an area of life in which you feel that Hashem is "asking too much" from you? See how you can turn the situation around and use it as a springboard to build your courage, loyalty, and love for Hashem.

85

You Don't Even Know

Hashem protects us against dangers we don't see.

Living in the times of Covid-19 has made us aware of the dangers we don't see with our eyes. Covid-19 is just one virus. How many other microscopic viruses and bacteria are floating around in the air, sitting on our doorknobs and towels or growing in our tuna sandwich? We wouldn't want to know. The amazing fact is that most of the time, most people do not become sick from them.

Let's consider a few other amazing scenarios: How many criminals are walking the streets? We don't know, because most of the time, most people are not victimized by them. How many bad drivers share the road with us? We don't know, because most of the time, most people are not involved in an accident. How many terrorists are plotting attacks against residents of Eretz Yisrael? We don't know, because most of the time, their plans do not come to fruition.

If every potential danger in our world were illuminated with a bright "WARNING! DANGER!" sign, we would live in such a high state of anxiety that we would never get out of bed. But Hashem doesn't allow that to happen; He shields us from dangers so that we do not even perceive them, allowing us to live our lives surrounded by a sense of order and safety. Certainly, sometimes the danger does come to pass, when Hashem determines that this is what must happen. In fact, this is how we know that these dangers exist. However, when we consider what is "out there," and how little we perceive of it, we realize that we are walking around in a protective bubble lovingly constructed for us by our Protector.

To help us keep in mind this "behind the scenes" protection, we have a mitzvah to remember each day the scheme of Balak and Bilaam, who set out to curse the Jewish people when they were encamped in the Wilderness. While Bilaam used his prophetic powers to pinpoint the exact moment that the Jewish people would be vulnerable to his curse, and Hashem wielded His unlimited power to protect them, the Jews went about their day as if nothing was happening.

When we remind ourselves of this scene, we also remind ourselves that while we are going about our business — eating our breakfast, sitting in class, *davening* Shacharis, walking the street — Hashem is taking care of us. So great is His care that He doesn't even want us to know about the danger. He is like a father who protects his children from frightening news and difficult challenges the family may be facing. There is no need to overwhelm them with worry because he is taking care of everything. A loving father wants his children to feel secure and confident.

Although the main feature of this type of protection is that we don't know about it, sometimes we find out. And when we do, our *emunah* soars to new heights. The following scenario illustrates just such an experience:

A True Story

Mrs. Davis was getting older and she knew that in another 12 years, she would want to sell her big house and move into a smaller one. She couldn't believe her good luck when Mr. Freund offered to buy her house and rent it out to her for the coming years. What a relief that would be for her — the house would be sold, she'd have all the money from the sale and yet, she'd be able to stay in her home until she was ready to move!

However, before buying a house, a buyer must have an engineer inspect it to make sure that the structure is strong and there are no hidden problems. Mr. Freund's engineer noticed that the house was slightly tilted. Mr.

Freund said he would buy the house only if Mrs. Davis took responsibility for fixing the problem. When Mrs. Davis looked into the matter, she found out that a main beam of the house had to be repaired; it would cost $12,000. She agreed to take care of it but didn't see any need to rush in to such a large expense. After all, she would be in the house for many years to come.

"No," insisted the buyer. "I want it done before I sign the contract."

Not wanting to lose the sale, Mrs. Davis went ahead. The contractor she hired called her over one day to see what he was doing. "Have you been waking up feeling dizzy lately?" he asked her. "I have!" she answered, wondering how he knew. He showed her an area behind the main beam. "This is a slow gas leak. You're lucky you called me now," the contractor said. "If this had gone on much longer, G-d forbid one day you might not have woken up at all."

Mrs. Davis never knew she was in danger, but Hashem did. And he protected her by sending her a buyer for her house who stubbornly insisted on a repair that was totally unrelated to the gas pipe. This, in the words of the *navi* Michah (6:5), is "in order to recognize the righteous acts of Hashem."

MAKE IT REAL:

If you start worrying about matters that are beyond your grasp, stop a moment and think: "Hashem is taking care."

86

"Is This Going to Be on the Test?"

Hashem wants us to get it right.

Why do students want to see the questions before they study for a test? The reason is that they will then be able to study the exact material they will need to know. With their answers prepared ahead of time, they will have a much better chance of earning a high score. With this incentive, sometimes students try to obtain a copy of the test before it's given.

Why don't teachers give out the test ahead of time if it will help the students perform better? It is because they want their students to study the material as a whole and gain an overall understanding. Parroting specific answers to specific questions doesn't demonstrate real knowledge.

The tests in life are no different. Hashem gives us a curriculum: we learn the mitzvos; we learn to recognize which character traits we should build and which we should work on overcoming; we learn to trust Him and try to do His will; we learn that He expects us to treat people with kindness and honesty. However, He doesn't tell us precisely how and when we will be tested on these lessons.

If we knew, *nisyonos* would be so much simpler! You might be in the middle of an argument with a sibling, ready to say something hurtful, when suddenly, a voice would ring out and say, "This is a test of your patience." You would have no trouble taking a deep breath and calming yourself down.

Or perhaps you've done something you shouldn't have and someone confronts you about it. You are about to lie when a sign appears overhead saying, "This is a test of your honesty." Although it might be hard to do, you'd tell the truth.

But Hashem doesn't want us to simply give the right answers. He wants us to become the right people. The lessons that will enable us to pass our tests in life must become part of us, and that means that we must build up our *emunah*, our *avodas Hashem*, and our *ahavas Yisrael* step by step; the *nisyonos* we face contain both the tests and the lessons.

When we begin to become the right people, we begin to recognize the test in the challenges that come along. This is the most valuable tool we have in our effort to become greater. As soon as we say to ourselves, "This is a test," our choice becomes clear — we feel Hashem watching, waiting to see what we will decide. We know it's a test and we know the right answer, and if we don't know, then we are motivated to seek out a wiser person to find out. When we learn to recognize the test, we are nearly guaranteed to pass.

Rabbi Menachem Cohen, one of the heads of Lev L'Achim, learned the power of knowing "this is a test" more than 60 years ago, as a student at the Ponevezh Yeshivah in Bnei Brak.

> *Rabbi Cohen sat in the Rosh Yeshivah's shiur for the first time when he witnessed an odd series of occurrences. The Rosh Yeshivah addressed a room packed with students, all listening intently to his words. In the middle of the shiur, a man entered the room and whispered into the Rosh Yeshivah's ear. The Rosh Yeshivah paused, replied and then continued teaching his students. A few minutes later, the scene repeated itself. Once again, the Rosh Yeshivah continued with his lesson.*
>
> *That night, he explained to his students what had happened. The yeshivah was in such dire financial straits that it had run out of money to buy food. "I called a friend yesterday, who told me that today, a wealthy man from America was going to visit various yeshivos to make large donations. He said he would send the man to me, and he showed up while I was teaching."*

The Rosh Yeshivah considered leaving the shiur to give the man his attention, but when he thought for a moment, he realized that this was a test. "Out of my entire day, this man has to come during the last 15 minutes of class? I asked my assistant to see if the man would wait, and he came back to tell me that the answer was no."

He stopped and thought for another moment. The yeshivah needed the money! However, he was more certain than ever that this was a test. Would he cause the entire yeshivah to lose out on their Torah learning to get a donation? He would not.

"To my surprise," the Rosh Yeshivah continued, "the wealthy man was still there when I concluded the class. He told me how impressed he was with our yeshivah. He said, 'If you weren't willing to stop for money, this must be a very serious place.'" The man gave a large donation, helping the yeshivah survive.

The test was about the Rosh Yeshivah's commitment to disseminating Torah and trusting Hashem to take care of the rest. But we need not be a Rosh Yeshivah to awaken ourselves to the fact that when our doubts are highest and our ideals are beginning to fray from the strain, *this is a test!*

MAKE IT REAL:

What situations tend to test you? Try helping yourself rise to the challenge by saying, in the midst of your confusion or irritation, "I know what this is. It's a test."

87

Did You Ever Really Pray?

It's not just something — it's everything.

It was a few weeks after Pesach, in April 2020, and Levi was in a situation he never would have believed could happen. His big bar mitzvah celebration had been canceled because of Covid-19. The newspapers and magazines were filled with stories about how wonderful it was that people were making do with simple backyard weddings and drive-by simchos, but to Levi, there was nothing wonderful about it at all. For months he had been imagining his big night. He was a popular boy with loads of friends, and he could just picture himself in the middle of the circle, dancing as the music pounded out the beat. Now his big night would take place in his backyard with a few close friends and his family. His grandparents and cousins wouldn't even be there. Why couldn't Hashem make this virus just go away?

We can imagine how difficult *davening* would be for a boy like Levi. He steps into *Shemoneh Esrei* and begins praising Hashem for His kindness and power, saying "*Melech Ozeir u'Moshia u'Magen* — the King, the One Who helps, Who saves and Who protects." He says that Hashem is the "*Rofei cholei amo Yisrael* — the Healer of His people," and "*Mevareich ha'shanim* — the One Who blesses the years" (with wealth). Meanwhile, a virus is taking over the world. Hashem doesn't seem to be healing, helping, saving, or protecting. On top of all that, Levi's father's business has been shut down because of the virus and the blessing of wealth also seems to be evaporating. Levi feels that the words of the *Shemoneh Esrei* are not connected to reality.

The missing piece in Levi's thinking is this: No matter where or when Hashem chooses to heal, grant wealth, save or protect us, it all comes from Him and only Him. He is the Sole Owner, Inventor, and Distributor of blessings. Although we may not see a particular blessing in our lives at the moment, Hashem is the only Source for it. When we pray to Him, we recognize this fact. For example, a person who is sick would not think, "*Rofei*? But I'm lying here miserable with fever!" Rather, he would think, "I might be sick right now, Hashem, but when I recover, it will only be because of You. You are the One and Only *Rofei*." All help, all protection, all salvation comes from just one address, even though Heaven may channel it through various people in our world.

One way to understand this idea is to compare Hashem's power to electricity: The power plant generates the electricity and sends it to substations, which send it through main wires and then smaller wires until it connects to our homes. If we walk into our house and the lights are off, this doesn't mean that there's no power. There is only one source of light and power in our house, and that is the power plant. Whether we are in the light or in the dark, that fact remains true.

When we pray, this understanding is at the heart of our effort. A real prayer is one that calls upon Hashem as the only address. We are not only asking Him to please send us intelligence, health, and wealth, or to please rebuild Yerushalayim and bring us Mashiach. Rather, we are also telling Him that we know, "You are the Only One Who can do this. We have no one else but You to rely on. Everything we want and need is in Your hands, and only You have the power to give it."

A real prayer is one we say with confidence that we've come to the right place. This puts a different feeling in our hearts as we pray. Imagine a small child in shul who is looking for the "candy man," but he's not quite sure which kindly older man it is. He goes to one and then another asking, "Can I have some candy please?" His feeling would be one of uncertainty; maybe this man has candy or maybe he doesn't. However, if the child knows exactly who to ask, his words might be the same but his feeling is very different. He knows that candy is in this man's pocket and that if the man deems it appropriate, he can hand it over to the little boy right then and there. This is the pure, simple certainty we need when we pray.

Often, when it seems as though our *hishtadlus* has not made any impact, Hashem's purpose is to bring us to this realization. He knows that we will pray a real prayer only when we truly feel that there is no other option. If our experience with Covid-19 has taught us anything, it is that nothing a human being says or does accomplishes anything until Hashem says, "It's time." All the power, healing, money, salvation, kindness, and blessing are Hashem's alone. When we pray with that belief firmly planted in our hearts, we have prayed a real prayer, and we will be answered.

The *navi* Yirmiyahu (17:7) states, "Blessed is the man who trusts in Hashem [for help]; then, Hashem will be his security (vouch for him)." We all want to be that fortunate person, but it takes work. We have to become actively involved in our prayers, finding thoughts of *emunah* that keep us focused and reminding ourselves as often as we can that Hashem is at the core of everything we see, do, and experience.

MAKE IT REAL:

Start your Shemoneh Esrei powerfully by putting special focus on the words, "Melech Ozeir u'Moshia u'Magen," remembering that any help and protection we experience comes only from Him.

88

Play to Win

Hashem carries us to the finish line.

How do you know what you're supposed to do with the life Hashem gave you? We know that every soul comes into the world with a mission, but the mission isn't written down neatly for us on a piece of paper. We have to find our way with the guidance of our parents, teachers, and Torah leaders.

We might wonder — are we meant to do something great? Start an organization that will help thousands of people? Develop an important new invention? Find the cure for a disease? Become a great Torah scholar? Most people will consider these ideas and say, "No...that's not for me. That takes superhuman ability." So how do human beings manage to achieve superhuman accomplishments?

Rav Dessler (*Michtav MeEliyahu,* Vol. 2) teaches that the more we persevere, the more Hashem helps us. When we run up against obstacles and the goal seems impossible to achieve, that's when our motivation should rev up to high gear. That's when we should pour every ounce of strength and creativity into finding our way around the problem. When we do this, we will be amazed to see that Hashem steps in and carries us to success.

Rav Nosson Tzvi Finkel, zt"l, the Rosh Yeshivah of Mir Yerushalayim, started life as a typical American Jewish boy from Chicago. He went to a Jewish day school, headed the student council, and played centerfield for the school baseball team. Nothing in his background would make someone think, "He's bound for greatness."

However, that is what he achieved. After going to Eretz Yisrael to learn with his great-uncle, Rav Leizer Yudel Finkel, who was the Mir Rosh Yeshivah, Rav Nosson Tzvi's greatness in learning began to shine. Eventually, he became the Rosh Yeshivah and took upon himself the task of building the yeshivah and raising money for its enormous budget.

The task wouldn't have been easy for anyone, but for Rav Nosson Tzvi, it required superhuman strength. That's because in 1980, he was diagnosed with Parkinson's disease, a muscle and nerve disease that causes a person to gradually lose control of his movements. Most people with Parkinson's are eventually confined to a bed and a wheelchair, but Rav Nosson Tzvi refused to give in. He traveled twice a year to Europe and America, visiting city after city to raise money for Mir. He learned constantly, with many chavrusas each day, including many Mir students. In his 20 years of running the yeshivah, it grew from 1,200 students to 7,600 — the largest Torah-learning institution in the world.

Rav Nosson Tzvi kept going when the going seemed impossible, and Hashem gave him the gift of success. No matter what our mission is in life, we will only find it and succeed at it if we grab every opportunity to do a mitzvah, to learn and to grow and to never be afraid to try a little harder.

MAKE IT REAL:

Think of a goal you've been reluctant to attempt, thinking that you don't have the ability to succeed. Map out a step-by-step plan toward that goal and take your first step.

89

Emunah in the Air

Look for miracles and you'll find them everywhere.

Shimon bought a saltwater fish tank and an interesting assortment of colorful saltwater fish. Setting up the tank was not an easy job, but he followed the directions and was soon enjoying the sight of his miniature underwater world. That is, until the next morning when he found one of his fish floating on its side, dead as could be. "Oh, well," he thought. "Maybe it wasn't a healthy fish."

However, it wasn't just that one fish. Every day for the next few days, he woke up to find a new "victim" floating atop the water. He went back to the store to complain.

"Could be the wrong pH level in the water," the storekeeper told him. "Or maybe you've got too much salt — or not enough. And are you sure the filter is set up correctly? The toxins build up quickly in the water."

Shimon was feeling a bit overwhelmed with all the details involved in maintaining the tank. "And this is just a 20-gallon tank," he thought. "How does Hashem keep all the fish alive in the ocean where there's so much pollution, no filter, and no one adjusting the pH and salt?"

The world of nature is really a series of miracles. This is what Rav Dessler explains in *Michtav MeEliyahu* (Vol. 1). He says that we see nature as "normal" because we are used to it. But imagine, he says, a person was standing near a grave when all of a sudden, the earth began to shake and someone rose out of the grave, dusted himself off, and walked away as if nothing ever happened. There would be no words to describe the amazement. Yet millions of times a day, a seed that is buried in the ground begins to break down and sends a little green shoot, a new bit of life, through the earth and into the sun. Hashem brings life from death, not only eventually when Mashiach comes, but every day. To us, however, it's nothing; we plant a seed and something grows. We don't see it as *techiyas hameisim* — restoring the dead to life — but that's what it is.

From the fine-tuned balance of our body's functions to the innate abilities of each creature to build a home and find its food, to the maintenance of giant planets in their orbits, our world defies explanation. Consider this: The atmosphere of the earth must contain 21 percent oxygen in order to sustain life. Too much would cause fires and explosions while too little would kill nearly every living thing. The balance of oxygen is maintained by people and animals inhaling it and exhaling carbon dioxide, while plants inhale carbon dioxide and exhale oxygen. Because the plants that grow in the ground cannot fulfill the function alone, Hashem spread algae across the ocean bed, which provide 80 percent of the world's oxygen.

These are all amazing facts, but we might still wonder, why does it matter? There are two powerful reasons: The first is that Hashem's precise design of the world is His way of telling us that He is here, that He is in complete control and that His wisdom is far, far beyond anything we could ever begin to understand. Anyone who recognizes the complexity of nature recognizes that the world has a Creator.

The second reason is that when we are mindful of what Hashem does for us each day as He maintains His creation in perfect working order, we feel gratitude. In *Modim,* we thank Hashem for "*nisecha shebechal yom imanu* — Your miracles that are with us every day. The more we recognize, the more we thank, and the more we know Hashem is here, caring for our every need. He has arranged the perfect scenery and props for us to play our role in the world. He is caring for us, extending His kindness toward us every minute. Knowing this keeps our *emunah* strong.

MAKING IT REAL:

Think of one aspect of nature that you find interesting and learn about it, keeping in mind that every detail is part of Hashem's design.

90

Check Your Emunah-Meter

Your heart tells the truth.

It was Chanukah time and Penina's family was gathered at her house. She hadn't seen her cousin Rachel all year. They had been close when their families lived near each other in Brooklyn, but ever since Rachel moved out of town, the girls found it hard to stay in touch. When Rachel's family car pulled up in front of Penina's house, she couldn't hold back. She burst through the front door into the frigid air and ran to her cousin for a long-awaited hug.

Soon, they were sitting together in the den, catching up on each other's news.

"How's it going in your new school?" Penina asked.

"Baruch Hashem. The principal is very tough, but it's OK. I guess I had it too easy before," Rachel answered, adding, "Baruch Hashem. Not to complain. It's just super-competitive."

"Oh," Penina sympathized. "That sounds hard."

"Well, it is what it is, right? It's just that it's hard for me to help my mother out when there's so much school pressure. And I don't get much sleep. I think what they expect from a bunch of teenage girls is pretty over-the-top," Rachel admitted. "But Baruch Hashem, I got into this school. Not everyone gets into a good high school."

If we listen to Rachel, we see one thing very clearly: She has learned the correct *emunah* perspective on life. She thanks Hashem even for her difficulties. She realizes that her situation could be worse and that she stands to benefit from a higher-level academic program. The words "*Baruch Hashem*" are always on her lips.

But it doesn't take an X-ray machine to see that inside Rachel, stress and anxiety are alive and well and growing each day. That is because the *emunah* she has installed so firmly in her mind is stuck there. It hasn't made its way into her heart, at least not strongly enough to affect her reaction to this challenge in her life.

There is a saying that the longest distance is from the head to the heart. What we know can be very different from what we feel. In fact, we often think of our emotions as an involuntary process, like the blinking of our eyes or the beating of our hearts. Can we really control our emotions?

The answer must be that we can. Otherwise, the Torah could not command us to feel certain feelings. For example, Hashem commanded Jewish soldiers who went out to war, "Do not fear them [the enemy]" (*Devarim* 20:1). Even though the Jews were outnumbered, and the enemy was charging at them with horses and chariots, they had to have faith that Hashem would hand them victory. Their assignment was to feel this with such certainty that they would not be afraid.

We can find many other examples of mitzvos that apply to our emotions. A Jew is commanded to love G-d and have compassion for orphans, widows, and converts. We are forbidden to be jealous of others and to hate others in our hearts. Since we know that the Torah does not command us to do things human beings are incapable of doing, we have the best proof possible that our emotions are within our control.

But that doesn't make it easy! To push that reservoir of *emunah* from our brain into our heart, we have to continually work on making it stronger. That means constantly feeding it with inspiring stories and *shiurim,* a little each day, and paying attention to the messages Hashem sends us every day of our lives. We won't notice every moment of *hashgachah pratis* and every blessing that comes our way, but with some focus, we will notice more — enough to assure ourselves again and again that Hashem is there for us, directing our steps and guiding us through our challenges.

As our inner *emunah* grows, we will notice that we don't become angry or frustrated as easily as we used to. When challenges arise, we won't feel our insides churning with stress. Little by little, we will become *baalei emunah,* people who live lives of peace and tranquility.

Besides continually strengthening our *emunah*, an equally important step is to recognize our own progress. For example, someone borrows an item from you and loses it. You know that a year ago, you would have blasted him, yelling, "That's how you take care of someone else's things? I should have known better than to loan it to you!" Now, however, you handle the situation calmly, thinking, "It looks like Hashem didn't want me to have that anymore." You might still work out a way for your friend to reimburse you for your loss, but there's no outrage involved. When you realize how far you've come, you'll feel confident in your ability to keep going. Just keep learning and trying to live what you learn. You're getting there!

MAKE IT REAL:

Think about challenges that have come up during the past couple of weeks. How much has your work on emunah affected the way you handled it?

91

When You're Not Feeling It

Store away your inspiring moments.

Did you ever open a *siddur* with all the best intentions, only to find that within moments, your mind has drifted so far away that you can't even remember how it got there? Surprisingly, this can happen even when we want very much to feel connected to Hashem. Perhaps there's some problem on our mind, or something we are deeply hoping for, and we know that our prayers are the only real solution. We want to have a great *tefillah* and still, we cannot focus.

What is happening? We ask ourselves, "How did you get all the way to *Shemoneh Esrei* without noticing that you said the *Shema*?" "How did you manage to plan your entire Shabbos while you're in the middle of praying?" It's as if one side of our brain is thinking and the other side is *davening*. This is disappointing enough under regular circumstances, but when we have serious business to bring before Hashem, how could we be so distracted? And yet, there we are, staring at the first words of *Shemoneh Esrei* with no idea how we got there.

When we want to connect to Hashem but our heart is simply not in it, the solution is to ask Hashem for help. We can tell Him, "I want to be close to You. I want to feel that You're here with me, listening to me *daven*, but I can't find the right feeling inside me. Please, Hashem, give me that feeling." In fact, we can have this intention when we begin *Shemoneh Esrei* with the words, "*Hashem, sifasai tivtach u'fi yagid tehillasecha* —

Hashem, open my lips and my mouth will declare Your praise." This is a prayer for the ability to pray, because the desire to pray comes from our *bechirah,* but the ability comes from Above.

Sometimes the obstacle to our prayers is a simple physical issue. For instance, if a person is very tired, he may not be able to concentrate. The same if he's sick or in pain. When the surroundings are uncomfortable or noisy, this too can quickly derail our prayers. However, sometimes our obstacle comes from a deeper place inside us. We may be tense or troubled and feel that Hashem is far from us just when we need Him most. That's when we need to be able to reach into our memory and relive a time when we felt so much closer.

We all have times when we feel, "Hashem, You're so good to me!" It could be when something we've prayed for finally happens, or when Hashem has saved us from danger. If our heart is open to *emunah,* we can find that feeling by simply focusing on the shower of goodness and gifts we are enjoying at this very moment. To have these memories at hand when we need them, we have to "take a snapshot" when they happen and stash those images away in our memory. Then, when we hit a low point, we can take out our snapshots and look at them, remembering how we felt. Hashem was with us then and He's with us still.

As the story below illustrates, Hashem can reach out a hand, *kav'yachol,* to draw us close even when He seems very far away. When we long for Him, He answers.

> *During the Holocaust, a Jewish boy named David Zeidelback was living with his family in Poland when the Germans invaded. He was only 13, but because he had blue eyes and blond hair like the Polish people, he was able to flee his hometown and hide among the non-Jews. He took a job working on a farm, and in this way he stayed safe.*
>
> *As the fall of 1942 began, David's mind turned to Rosh Hashanah and Yom Kippur. He became filled with longing to sit by his father in shul and hear the chazzan's stirring prayers. How he wished he knew what days the Yamim*

Tovim would be! Then at least he could try to say some prayers, although he knew very little by heart.

Just as he was thinking about this, his boss sent him into town to buy groceries. When he arrived at the market, he asked the grocer for a half-pound of salt and a pound of sugar. His heart nearly stopped beating when he saw the grocer rip pages from a sefer to make the cones into which he poured the salt and sugar. The Nazis had confiscated piles of sefarim and distributed them for all sorts of unholy purposes, as if they were nothing more than old newspapers.

David didn't allow his face to show his shock. He could not risk being discovered as a Jew. But as soon as he was alone, he opened the paper cones to see which holy sefer had been so terribly desecrated. The pages were from a Rosh Hashanah prayer book, and included the prayer "Unesaneh Tokef," one of the most moving prayers of both Rosh Hashanah and Yom Kippur. David read each word, pouring his troubles and hopes into his prayers, his heart filled with thanks to Hashem for giving him the words to say.

With the help of Hashem's loud and clear message, "I'm with you!" David survived the war. He later said that whenever he felt down, he took out his "snapshot" of that incredible moment when he opened up a cone of salt and found Hashem's love.

MAKE IT REAL:

Start collecting your own snapshots — your own images of moments when you felt Hashem's love and care. Take them out and look at them whenever you have a hard time connecting to Him.

92

It Fits Perfectly!

Hashem tailors the reward to the deed.

Understanding how Hashem deals with us requires a quick lesson on the stock market: When someone buys stock in a company, he's buying a little piece of ownership in the company. As the company grows, his stock becomes more valuable. Meanwhile, as the company's income increases, the company occasionally sends its stockholders a cash payment — their portion of the profit. That's called a dividend.

What does that have to do with Hashem? It explains how we benefit in this world for a mitzvah even though the actual reward is reserved for us in Heaven. As we serve Hashem with learning, mitzvos, and *chesed*, the value of our stock goes up. However, Hashem sends us the dividends in this world. He shows us that He counts us as one of His investors; He has our address and sends us a sign that our business is prospering. Through these dividends — Hashem's blessings and protection — we are encouraged to keep investing. It pays!

To make sure that we clearly see the connection between our mitzvos and the dividends they earn, Hashem rewards us *middah k'neged middah* (measure for measure) with a benefit we can trace directly to our good deed. The Torah even spells out some of these dividends. For example, the Gemara (*Rosh Hashanah* 16a) tells us to celebrate the *Simchas Beis Ha'shoeivah* on Succos because Succos is the time of year that Hashem determines how much rain will fall. Doing a mitzvah with water brings the blessing of plentiful water. In the same way, we bring the *omer* (an offering of barley) on the first day of Chol HaMoed, in the spring, because that is when Hashem decides how much grain the world will have. Even so, when rain and grain are plentiful and we enjoy the abundance, we are not "eating up" our reward for these mitzvos; the reward remains whole in Heaven. We are eating the dividends.

Hashem draws this clear bright line between our mitzvos and our dividends to reveal a glimpse of Himself to us. We can easily ignore the connection if we're not looking for it. However, if we look for it, we will find it everywhere. When we do, we become more confident that Hashem is taking note of all our efforts and values us as "investors" in His creation. The key to becoming aware of the *middah k'neged middah* rewards Hashem sends us is to use a long-range lens. These rewards do not usually come on the heels of the mitzvah — that would take away our *bechirah* just as certainly as if lightning struck us when we did an *aveirah*. Rather, the rewards come some time later: it might be in a week, in years, or even in a different generation. However, to a person viewing the world through an *emunah* lens, the connection is clear, as in the story below, told by Rabbi Elimelech Biderman:

> *Yaakov Halpern was a wealthy man who appreciated fine watches. One day, he ordered an expensive new watch that would take about four months to make. During that time, he gradually set aside the money to pay for the watch — 200,000 shekels (about $50,000). The months passed by and the dealer called to tell Yaakov that his watch was ready to be picked up. However, Yaakov was out of town at the time; he wouldn't be able to pick it up until he returned.*
>
> *A few hours after the dealer called, Yaakov received another call. This was from a man who was collecting money to help a family whose house had burned down. He was trying to raise 400,000 shekels to rebuild the home and hoped that Yaakov could make a large contribution. Although Yaakov was wealthy, all his money was invested at that time. The only ready cash he had was the money he had saved for the watch. He*

told the caller that he would think about the situation and get back to him.

And Yaakov thought: "That watch was manufactured specifically for me. I can't just say, 'never mind.' On the other hand, how can I enjoy a luxury watch when I know there's a homeless family that could use the money?" He decided to call the dealer and see if it would be possible to cancel his order.

"Actually, I have a waiting list of people for this watch," the dealer said. "We could easily sell it to someone else." Yaakov had his answer. He gave up the watch and sent 200,000 shekels to the family.

About three years later, wildfires were breaking out all over Eretz Yisrael. On a Thursday night in November, the fires spread to Moshav Beis Meir near Yerushalayim, where Yaakov lived. He and his son, who was with him at the time, had to flee from the oncoming fire, abandoning his large, beautiful house and everything in it. On Friday morning, they returned to assess the damage.

The sight they beheld was shocking. The fire had completely destroyed the house next door to the Halperns'. Then, as if blocked by a stone wall, the fire had stopped at the property line. Not even the delicate new trees he had planted on the border of the property were singed.

We are not capable of understanding Hashem's reasoning. Why did the other homeowners have to suffer loss? Surely they, too, had merits that could protect them. These are calculations we must leave to Heaven. But one calculation Hashem made very clear. The man who helped a family that had lost their home to fire received his dividend, *middah k'neged middah,* when his own home was saved from fire.

MAKE IT REAL:

Think about the mitzvos you are especially careful to do, or those that have been especially challenging. Can you find any middah k'neged middah dividends for those mitzvos?

93

A Blessing for You

With each berachah we make, we remind ourselves: "There He is!"

Imagine that every day, you thanked your parents for 100 things they do for you. You'd get out of bed and say to your mother, "Thanks for choosing that mattress for me, Ma. It's really comfortable." You'd see your father leaving for work and say, "Thanks for working so hard to support me, Daddy." You wouldn't just thank them for what they've done for you recently, but for everything they do — especially the things they do day in and day out.

No doubt, your parents would appreciate the appreciation, but imagine how such a routine would change *you*. The more you would notice what they do for you and thank them, the more loved and cared for you would feel. After just one day, you'd feel as though you were the most pampered child on earth. In addition, every thank-you would spotlight just a little bit more of your parents' outstanding love and *chesed*, as well as their ability to provide for you.

This is the power of a *berachah*. The Torah instilled in the life of a Jew a system that reminds us constantly of Hashem's love, His *chesed,* and His power to provide us with all we need. When we say a *berachah,* the experience can be like opening a small window into *Shamayim* that lets a little bit more of Hashem's light into our life. This, says the *Alei Shur,* helps us defeat the doubts and problems that arise when we forget that

Hashem is a reality. Each time we say a blessing, we remind ourselves, "There He is!" and "There He is again!"

Not only does reciting a *berachah* acknowledge Who is caring for us at every moment, but it also opens new channels for more *berachah* to come into the world. Hashem's entire purpose for giving us abundance in the world is to awaken us to His Presence and create a connection with us. It makes sense then that the more we recognize His gifts and thank Him for them, the more gifts He will send, because they are serving their purpose. We can easily imagine this on a human level: You have an aunt who lives on the other side of the country and she sends you gifts for every Yom Tov and birthday to show that she's thinking of you. Your appreciation is what makes her effort worthwhile. If you don't think of her when you enjoy the gift, what is the point?

The power of our *berachos* to bring more *berachah* into the world came to light in the days of Dovid HaMelech. At that time there was a terrible plague, and the Jewish people needed merit to bring it to an end. Through *ruach hakodesh,* Dovid HaMelech saw that if the people would say 100 *berachos* each day, they would have the merit they needed. They followed his instructions and the plague quickly ended. The *Orchos Chaim* adds that a person who says 100 *berachos* a day is guaranteed a share in *Olam Haba.* Such a person, says Rabbi Yehudah Tzadka, will have said 2.5 million *berachos* by the time he reaches the age of 70!

By now, you might be wondering how all this goodness and blessing can come from those short lines you mumble before eating, or the 18 blessings you speed through while saying *Shemoneh Esrei.* The answer is that the benefits we are discussing do not come to us unless we focus on the *berachah's* words and say them with a real spark of gratitude. Many people have taken on a commitment to say their *berachos* clearly and with feeling, only to find themselves lapsing back into autopilot. However, this seemingly insurmountable problem can be solved in a matter of seconds.

Rabbi Tzadka tells us how. We simply pause for a moment after the words *Baruch Atah Hashem* and then again after the words *Elokeinu Melech ha'olam.* One person who took this advice adds a further, powerful strategy. During the first pause, remind yourself that by saying "*Atah,*" you are now speaking directly to Hashem. During the second pause, remind yourself that the King Who rules the entire universe — picture the galaxies and tiny Planet Earth — is personally reaching down into your little corner of the world and tenderly caring for you. With just a flash of an image in your mind as you take these pauses, your *berachos* will become alive.

> *Rav Yisrael Salanter was in Paris. While walking on the street, he realized that he was thirsty. He stopped at a café and asked for water, but the waiter told him he had to sit down at a table and be served. He sat down, received the water, said "Shehakol" and drank. Then the bill came. It was an astronomical price for a simple glass of water.*
>
> *Wanting to understand why the bill was so high, the Rav asked the waiter. "Well, sir, you are not just paying for water in a place like this. You are paying for the atmosphere, the fine art, the beautiful view. You're paying for the whole package."*
>
> *This information delighted Rav Salanter. When he returned to his yeshivah, he gathered his students and told them that his berachos had been strengthened by a new appreciation for Hashem's kindness. "Even if we were drinking water in a jail cell, we would have to make a berachah," he said. "But Hashem gives us water in a magnificent world surrounded by our loved ones. When we say 'Shehakol,' we're not just thanking Hashem for the drink, but for the whole package."*

Every new insight into Hashem's kindness brings us to a higher level of *emunah* and happiness. *Berachos* give us 100 opportunities a day to reach a new rung on the ladder.

MAKE IT REAL:

Whether you've never tried it before or have tried and given up, begin to work on increasing your focus on berachos. Use Rabbi Tzadka's advice for a few pre-selected times each day and gradually build from there.

94

You Won't Wait One Extra Second

So much anxiety comes from wondering when.

When we're waiting for an answer to our prayers, our patience can begin to run out. We know Hashem has what we need and we know that we really need it; what is He waiting for? Instead of thinking that "He hasn't answered me yet," we begin thinking, "I'm praying but He's not answering." Our fear is that perhaps He will never answer.

For us to maintain our *emunah* and keep praying with sincere belief that Hashem will help us, we have to remember that "not yet" doesn't mean "never." We don't know when the time is right. In our view, the greatest kindness would be to answer us now: solve our problem, fulfill our need, and let us move forward. However, Hashem knows when the time is right. At that moment, He will answer us. As the verse in *Ashrei* says, "You give them their food in its proper time." The story below illustrates this idea in action:

> *A man who is now a Rabbi in Eretz Yisrael was once a non-religious young man living in Brooklyn. One night, back in those days, he was out with a group of friends when the watch he was wearing mysteriously disappeared. No one in his group seemed to know what happened. Perhaps he had taken it off and forgotten about it. It was an expensive watch, and now it was gone.*
>
> *Not too long after this experience, he went to Eretz Yisrael and began learning Torah. Eventually, he became*

a rebbi in a yeshivah there. One Thursday, he realized that his bank account was empty. He had nothing with which to prepare Shabbos, and six boys from his yeshivah were coming for the Friday-night meal. He contacted his brother in America, who offered to send money into his account. However, on Friday morning the money wasn't there, and it was already Shabbos in America. The rebbi was stuck.

He began walking to the grocery store anyway, praying that Hashem would somehow enable him to buy what he needed. When he got to the store, he was surprised to bump into Danny, one of his old friends from New York, who was visiting Israel with his wife. As soon as the two friends were finished greeting each other, Danny's face turned serious. "I have a confession to make," he said. "I was the one who stole your watch that night eight years ago. Since then, I've become religious and I've been praying that I would be able to find you and pay you back. I'm so happy to see you! I know that watch was expensive, and I want to pay back every dollar. Tell me how much it cost." Danny went to the bank, withdrew the cash, and handed it to the rebbi.

For both men, Hashem's timing was perfect. There's little doubt that with the rebbi's small income and high expenses, he would have had to spend the money on some other expense if it had come to him earlier in the week. Instead, Hashem put it into his hand when he needed it most. Hashem took Danny's prayer to be able to do *teshuvah* and the rebbi's prayer for money to make Shabbos and coordinated them as only He could.

So much of our anxiety in life comes from wondering "when." Living with *emunah* enables us to stop aggravating ourselves with that question. Whether we're waiting for something as trivial as a bus or as significant as a *shidduch,* there is only one answer. Everything goes according to Hashem's timing. When the moment is right, when we can most benefit from and most appreciate the thing for which we are praying, that is when it will come. Meanwhile, our job is to keep praying with full trust that Hashem hears every word we say. It could be that one more prayer is all we need to make "now" the right time.

MAKE IT REAL:

The next time you bump into "just the person you needed to see," think about the timing. Had you or he showed up any earlier or later, you may not have met.

95

An Audience of One

A humble person is never insulted.

How do teachers and parents get young children excited about all the hard work of learning and growing up? If you think back to elementary school, you'll probably remember learning contests, *chesed* contests, charts, stickers, candies, and prizes. To get children motivated, we turn work into a game. That little flame of competition burning in their heart pushes them forward like gasoline fuels an engine.

But the true goal is that once children develop the skills they need, and they understand the importance of what they are learning, they will no longer need contests to motivate them. They will want to learn Torah, do mitzvos, and help others because they want to please Hashem. That's the ideal. In between the child's view and the ideal view is the average person's view. Almost everyone enjoys a little recognition. Praise feels good, even to an 80-year-old man. Few people are so humble that they run away from the spotlight.

However, for many people, recognition isn't just "the frosting on the cake" — it's the cake itself. If they do a favor for someone, their satisfaction isn't complete unless they tell others about it and hear about how kind they are. If they give money, they expect honor in return. In learning, too, many students are not happy with their achievements unless others recognize them as a top student. Some people cannot enjoy their wealth unless others know how wealthy they are. They tell everyone how much they spent on their new shoes, just to make sure that no one misses the point.

Now that many people belong to social media groups like WhatsApp, this need for recognition has grown into a monster. People constantly publicize what they're doing, where they're going, what they bought and dozens of other details, all with the goal of having their contacts "like" or comment on what they've posted. If we look at this objectively, it is rather sad. It's as if millions of adults spend their days begging their friends, "Like me! Like me! *Please like me!*" When someone is ignored, he feels miserable.

People who are so dependent on others' approval are stuck in a trap that they've built themselves. When people fail to recognize them, they feel like failures. They are often hurt and angry. Their happiness is in other people's control.

A Jew with *emunah,* however, is free from all that. He is the freest person in the world. This is because he knows that he is receiving all the recognition he needs, and the only recognition that really counts. The *navi* Michah (6:8) advises us "to walk humbly with your G-d," which means that we should be modest and quiet about our achievements because Hashem is with us. He is right there alongside us as we help out a friend or sweat over our learning or give our *ma'aser* to a good cause.

By living this way, we build true *anivus,* the trait of humility, which the *Iggeres HaRamban* calls "the greatest of all good character traits." A humble person saves himself from all the detrimental traits caused by chasing after honor and recognition. He doesn't feel jealous when someone else receives credit. He doesn't become impatient when people get in the way of his plans. He isn't angered by others' comments.

The Torah tells us that the verse, "Moshe was the humblest of men" (*Bamidbar* 12:3), is an interruption in the conversation between Miriam and Aharon, which was considered *lashon hara* about Moshe. The reason this line is interjected into the middle of their conversation is to tell us that Moshe was not the least bit insulted by the words being spoken about him.

Humility can only develop in a person who has *emunah*. That is because someone with *emunah* realizes that all his strengths, talents, and good fortune come to him from Hashem. He feels grateful rather than proud. Realizing that Hashem has invested in him, he knows that he is obligated to use all Hashem has given him wisely, to do good in the world. When he does a mitzvah or a *chesed*, he is acting only as Hashem's agent. From that point of view, applause is not only unneeded, but it is unwanted as well. Humility is the common trait of all truly great people, an unmistakable sign that they live their lives in Hashem's Presence. As the story below illustrates, we discover just how great a person is when we discover how humble he is:

> *Reb Itzele Peterberger was a great Torah scholar. He was invited to a conference of Gedolim that included the most famous Torah figures of his time; the Beis HaLevi (Rav Yosef Dov Soloveitchik) and his son, Rav Chaim, were among them. At one point, the Beis HaLevi presented a complex question on Gemara. A fierce debate ensued, but no one could find a solution. The Beis HaLevi then presented a brilliant solution. When he finished, he asked his son to present his answer, which was even more distinctive.*
>
> *Later that day, the Beis HaLevi began to wonder why Reb Itzele, who was known for his sharp intellect, had not offered an answer to the question. He withdrew the Pri Yitzchak, authored by Reb Itzele, from his bookshelf and began scanning the pages that discussed the topic of that day's question. He was astonished to see that Reb Itzele had posed the same question and given both the Beis HaLevi's answer and Rav Chaim's as well. But he had sat silently, not wishing to turn the spotlight away from the Beis HaLevi and onto himself.*

The more we recognize that Hashem sees what we're doing, the less we need others' reassurance that we count.

MAKE IT REAL:

Start learning to free yourself from the need for recognition. The next time you do something you feel proud of, tell yourself, "It's just between me and Hashem."

96

Bigger Than You Can Imagine

Small mitzvos are worth so much more than we realize.

In our world, items that are available in large quantities are usually worth less than items that are rare. A thousand diamond chips won't come near the value of one 10-carat diamond. A thousand printed pictures are worth far less than one hand-painted masterpiece.

This might give us the impression that mitzvos we do often are worth less than the big, difficult mitzvos we do rarely. We might think that our daily struggle over a few lines of Gemara is worth less than the brilliant insight of a *talmid chacham,* or that the small deeds we do each day to help our parents are worth less than a great celebration we make to honor their birthday or anniversary.

This impression, however, is wrong. We cannot fathom the value of even the smallest mitzvos we do. Each mitzvah is packed with potential for extraordinary, indescribable reward. If we make the most of the mitzvah by doing it with enthusiasm, we increase its value even more. While no one has gone to *Shamayim* and come back with a report that confirms this idea, Rav Shach tells a story that gives us an insight. It comes from a manuscript that was found in Vilna:

> *The Vilna Gaon's mother and her friend, both elderly women, made a deal with each other. Whoever died first would come to the other in a dream and tell her what*

the Next World was like. One woman passed away (we don't know which one) and soon appeared to her friend as they had agreed.

"I'm not permitted to tell you anything about where I am," she said. "But I can tell you this: You and I once went together to visit someone who was sick, and we couldn't find the house. I was ready to give up when you suddenly spotted it. You pointed at the house with such excitement. You cannot imagine how much more reward you are getting for that mitzvah than I am, all because of your enthusiasm."

What does this teach us? It shows that Hashem prizes our effort and enthusiasm for serving Him. On a merit scale of 1 to 10, 1 being "saying a *berachah* while half-asleep" and 10 being "saving a life," we might place "pointing excitedly at a house" at about 2. However, as Rav Shach teaches, it is infinitely precious. That means that paying attention to the "small" mitzvos we do, and doing them with a sense of happiness and purpose, can earn us vast rewards. The truth is that we do not necessarily have to do something more; we need only invest more into what we are already doing. If we are doing a *chesed*, we can put more heart into it. If we are learning, we can add more focus. Sometimes the "extra" can be a finishing touch on that which we are already doing — a little extra kindness, a smile and a kind word to go with a favor, an extra five minutes of learning, real *kavannah* for a *berachah*. We're doing it anyway!

How do we know this is worthwhile? Even if people don't come to us in a dream from the Next World, sometimes we can see the evidence right here in the physical world. Small things we do can make an enormous impact, as this true story illustrates:

A TRUE STORY

Many years ago, a family living in New York was unable to support itself. Things became so difficult that the father asked his oldest son, Jacob, to go door to door seeking handouts in various Jewish neighborhoods. The son did as he was asked, accepting a dollar or two from those who were kind enough to give. Meanwhile, Jacob held on to a dream of becoming a doctor one day. His parents took a few dollars each week from the money he collected and set it aside for his education.

One day, Jacob knocked on the door of the Gross home. The daughter, Sarah*, answered the door. She wanted to give, but when she checked her pockets, she found that she had no money on her. Meanwhile, her father yelled from upstairs, "Sarah, who's there?"*

When she told him that it was someone collecting tzedakah, he yelled angrily that he had had enough of "these collectors" and she should not give him money. Even so, it was a freezing cold night and the girl felt bad for Jacob. She invited him in and gave him a cup of hot cocoa. Years later, when remembering that moment, he said, "At the time, I thought it was the most delicious drink I had ever had."

Twenty-two years passed, and Jacob had achieved his dream. He was a top doctor and the head of his department in a hospital. One day, a patient named Sarah Marcus was admitted with a rare, dangerous disease. He saw on the patient's records that her father's name was Abe Gross. It was the girl who had given him that cup of cocoa, and now he had the chance to return the kindness. Jacob took care of Sarah as if she were his own sister. He paid for expensive treatments that her insurance didn't cover and flew in a doctor who specialized in her condition. After a long year of treatment, Sarah, baruch Hashem, recovered. When she was ready to leave the hospital, her husband was given the lengthy, detailed bill for the hospital's services, which added up to hundreds of thousands of dollars. At the bottom, it said, "Paid in full with a cup of cocoa."*

Like Sarah's small, thoughtful act of giving Jacob a cup of cocoa, our small deeds bring us rewards we could never imagine. Sometimes we see it in life; sometimes we don't. But with *emunah,* we can be sure that the reward awaits us.

MAKE IT REAL:

Take one mitzvah you do regularly and increase its value by injecting it with more enthusiasm or putting a "finishing touch" on it.

97

Keep Asking Until You Know

The biggest threat to emunah is fear of asking questions.

As we come to the last lesson on *emunah,* we have learned that it is the core of everything we do — not only in Torah and mitzvos, but in all the activities of our day. We've looked at *emunah* in 96 different ways and read dozens of stories that show us how it imparts us in real life. After all of this, we can sum up the meaning of *emunah* in just two words: "Hashem exists." The rest of our belief comes from understanding Who Hashem is and what He does:

- He is the One and Only Power; nothing happens unless He wills it to be.
- He knows everything and He is perfect.
- He loves us more than any human being can love us.
- He is purely good and only wants to give us goodness.
- When we put these pieces together, we emerge with one true way to look at life: Whatever happens to us is Hashem's will, and therefore, it is perfect and good for us.

The more firmly we believe this, the greater our love and trust in Hashem will be. That translates into serving Him with more sincerity. If we truly believe that Torah and mitzvos are our way to fulfill what Hashem wants of us, and that He sees and treasures our service, we will always strive to serve Him with more energy.

Imagine how someone would feel about staying home with cell phones and computers shut for 25 hours every week if he wasn't doing it for Hashem? How and why would he agree to stay out of all the world's most famous restaurants and limit himself to the handful of kosher ones? Who would get up an hour early every day and go to shul to recite verse after verse of Hebrew words? Why would anyone spend the majority of his or her school day studying ancient texts? Without Hashem at the center of all this, none of it makes sense. Even if someone is brought up in a religious home, without *emunah,* he or she will have a hard time holding on to the mitzvos.

Every thinking person, however, has questions. The answers we receive when we ask our questions often raise even more questions. However, the most dangerous threat to our *emunah* is not questions. Rather, it's being embarrassed or afraid to ask. The evidence that Hashem exists and is involved with our life is everywhere; it's in the dozens of stories told in this book and the many hundreds of other stories told in other books. In addition, our *sefarim* and the Torah itself provide abundant proof. Still, *emunah* remains a challenge because we cannot see Hashem!

When doubts arise, when things don't make sense, we are obligated to find someone we trust and ask that person our questions. The only other choice is a life of "faking it," which will only put more distance between ourselves and our *neshamah,* sapping the vitality from our *avodas Hashem* until it is nearly lifeless. On the other hand, hearing the truth invigorates our *neshamah* and revives our connection to Hashem, as we see in this story from the *sefer Emunah Sheleimah*. It is told by the daughter of a well-known Rabbi. Her story starts after she graduated from a prestigious elementary school and high school, and then entered a prominent seminary in Eretz Yisrael:

> *"I didn't feel like I belonged there," she said. "I had so many questions about religion and G-d, but I never asked them because I was too embarrassed. I didn't feel connected to Judaism — I was just going through the motions."*
>
> *That year, a friend invited her to join her in a summer*

camp in Eretz Yisrael. Her parents agreed to allow her to go, but her friend ended up backing out because of a family simchah. The girl found herself in a place where no one knew her, and the feeling was liberating.

"I could be myself," she said. "No one would judge me."

One night, a speaker named Rabbi Braun came to discuss Jewish philosophy. The girl saw her chance to ask her questions. She asked one question after another until Rabbi Braun said, "You don't believe there is a Hashem, correct?" The girl admitted that he was right.

"Don't worry. I will stay here as long as it takes to convince you," the Rabbi assured her.

That night, this girl and many of her fellow campers peppered the Rabbi with questions and he answered every one of them, supported by powerful proof. The girls followed up on their questions until they were satisfied.

"Now," said the girl, "I am happy to say that I follow Torah and mitzvos to the best of my ability with excitement, with feeling, with a real connection to Hashem."

Belief in Hashem is the heart of our life as Jews. Surely, in the physical sense, if we experience an uncomfortable feeling in our heart, we are foolish to ignore it. Likewise, we must keep the heart of our *avodas Hashem* strong and healthy, pumping energy and *simchah* into every moment of our life.

MAKE IT REAL:

If you have trouble feeling that Hashem is a reality, find a book or shiur on the fundamentals of emunah. Most of all, never think these questions make you a "bad Jew." Remember that it's our obligation to ask and learn until we recognize the truth.

This volume is part of
THE ARTSCROLL® SERIES
an ongoing project of
translations, commentaries and expositions on
Scripture, Mishnah, Talmud, Midrash, Halachah,
liturgy, history, the classic Rabbinic writings,
biographies and thought.

For a brochure of current publications
visit your local Hebrew bookseller
or contact the publisher:

Mesorah Publications, ltd

313 Regina Avenue
Rahway, New Jersey 07065
(718) 921-9000
www.artscroll.com